TRUE TO LIFE

STARTER

Stephen Slater
Simon Haines

PERSONAL STUDY
WORKBOOK

CAMBRIDGE
UNIVERSITY PRESS

PUBLISHED BY THE PRESS SYNDICATE OF THE UNIVERSITY OF CAMBRIDGE
The Pitt Building, Trumpington Street, Cambridge, United Kingdom

CAMBRIDGE UNIVERSITY PRESS
The Edinburgh Building, Cambridge CB2 2RU, UK
40 West 20th Street, New York, NY 10011–4211, USA
10 Stamford Road, Oakleigh, VIC 3166, Australia
Ruiz de Alarcón 13, 28014 Madrid, Spain
Dock House, The Waterfront, Cape Town 8001, South Africa

http://www.cambridge.org

First published 1998
Third printing 2001

Printed in the United Kingdom at the University Press, Cambridge

ISBN 0 521 59577 0 Personal Study Workbook
ISBN 0 521 59578 9 Class Book
ISBN 0 521 59576 2 Teacher's Book
ISBN 0 521 59575 4 Class Cassette Set
ISBN 0 521 59574 6 Personal Study Cassette
ISBN 0 521 59573 8 Personal Study Audio CD

CONTENTS

HI AND BYE

Write responses to the greetings.

Listen to 4 conversations. <u>Underline</u> the words on the recording.

1. A: Good <u>morning.</u>
   B: Good morning.

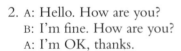

2. A: Hello. How are you?
   B: I'm fine. How are you?
   A: I'm OK, thanks.

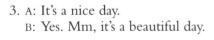

3. A: It's a nice day.
   B: Yes. Mm, it's a beautiful day.

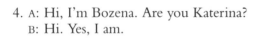

4. A: Hi, I'm Bozena. Are you Katerina?
   B: Hi. Yes, I am.

3 Correct the words

Choose letters from the box. Correct the words 1–6.

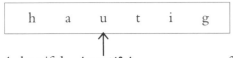

h	a	u	t	i	g

1. beatiful   *beautiful*

2. eigt

3. meetin

4. frend

5. techer

6. leter

4 How are you?

Complete the questions.

1. A: H *ow*   *are*   *you* ?

   B: Fine, thanks.

2. A: .... Juan?

   B: No, I'm Jaime.

3. A: I'm fine, thanks. How .... y........?

   B: I'm OK, thank you.

4. A: W............................ n............?

   B: Helena.

   A: .... late?

   B: No, you're not.

Listen and check your answers.

5 How about a coffee at ten?

Complete this note to a new student.

Hi (1) ...., I'm (2) ....
How are you?
It's a (3) .... day. How about a
(4) .... at (5) .... ?
My phone number is (6) ....
Bye
(7) ....

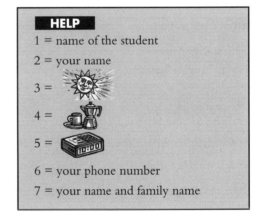

HELP
1 = name of the student
2 = your name
3 =
4 =
5 =
6 = your phone number
7 = your name and family name

6 It's a drink

Put the examples from the box with the correct group word.

a park	tea	K	How are you?
eight	Laurence	Hi.	

Group word	Example
a drink	....
a place	....
a greeting	*Hi.*
a question	....
a number	....
a letter	....
a name	....

C D E F G
B 4 5 6 7 H
A 2 3 8 I
Z 1 9 J
Y 10 K
X L
W M
V N
U O
T S R Q P

Write the answers.

A a is letter number one (1)

J j is letter number .... (10)

C c is letter number .... (.........)

.... is letter number seven (7)

E e is letter number .... (.........)

.... is letter number nine (9)

.... is letter number .... (4)

A ▭ Listen and write the 5 final letters from the box in this conversation.

t	d	s	t	p

ELENA: Are you OK?

SANDOR: Yes, thank.s... (1)

ELENA: I'm Elena.

SANDOR: Pleased to mee..... (2) you. I'm Sandor.

ELENA: Nice day.

SANDOR: Mm, and the coffee is goo...... (3)

ELENA: Mm, it is.

SANDOR: It's a grea..... (4) coffee sho...... (5)

ELENA: Mm, it's nice.

B ▭ Listen again and respond.

9 Visual dictionary

Complete the visual dictionary for Unit 1 on page 71.

Lost in time – EPISODE 1 ▭▭

It's one in the morning. A hotel room in Prague.
A phone rings.

JANA: *Yes?*
MAN: *How are you, Jana?*
JANA: *Pardon?*
MAN: *Is that Jana?*
JANA: *No.*
MAN: *Jana and Pierre?*
JANA: *No, no … I'm … I'm Helena. Goodbye.*

MAN: *Is Pierre OK?*
JANA: *What's your name?*
MAN: *Is Pierre OK?*
JANA: *Sorry, I'm Helena.*
MAN: *OK 'Helena', is Pierre there?*
JANA: *What's your name, please?*

JANA: *Pierre.*
PIERRE: *Mm … what is it? Is it late? I'm hungry.*
JANA: *Mm, it's nearly two in the morning. How about a hot dog?*
PIERRE: *All right … Mum, are you OK?*
JANA: *Yes I'm OK.*

But Jana and Pierre are not OK.

WELCOME!

---

1 Matching

Match a question with the right answer.

1. What's your first name?

2. What's your family name?

3. Can you spell that, please?

4. What's your address?

5. Is that a restaurant?

6. Is Ankara the capital of Australia?

7. Where's Ankara?

8. Is Sydney in Australia?

9. Where's my room?

10. Can I have a coffee, please?

a. Yes, it is.

b. Yes, it's B-R-O-W-N.

c. Yes, of course.

d. It's in Turkey.

e. It's on the fifth floor.

f. 17, Old Road, Liverpool.

g. No, it's a hotel.

h. It's Peter.

i. No, it isn't.

j. It's Brown.

---

2 One, two, three

Fill in the missing words.
Follow the example.

Example: *one hotel*   *two* **hotels**

1. one man   three ....

2. one country   six ....

3. one woman   two ....

4. one bus   two ....

5. one floor   five ....

6. one person   four ....

A Fill the gaps with the correct prepositions.

in	of	on	to	at

1. Welcome ....*to*...... Madrid.

2. Madrid is .... Spain.

3. Madrid is the capital .... Spain.

4. We are .... the Hilton Hotel.

5. You are .... Room 15.

6. Room 15 is .... the fourth floor.

B Where's Bob? Write sentences about Bob.

Example: *He's in Room 37.*

1. ....

3. ....

2. ....

4. ....

1. Where Bombay?   *Where is Bombay?* ....

2. What's that's?   ....

3. France and Italy is in Europe.   ....

4. My room is on the six floor.   ....

5. Can tell me your first name?   ....

6. Can help you?   ....

7. Excuse. Is this your key?   ....

8. No, it is.   ....

5 Buildings, rooms and people

Put the words in the box into the right groups.

bar	friend	guide	gym
hotel	rest room	restaurant	
shop	station	student	teacher

People
friend ....

....

....

....

Buildings

....

....

....

....

Rooms

....

....

....

....

6 Numbers and letters of the alphabet

A Find the letters and write the name.

First line

Second line

Third line

1. The sixth letter in the third line ..... *N* .....
2. The third letter in the first line ....
3. The ninth letter in the second line ....
4. The second letter in the second line ....
5. The ninth letter in the first line ....
6. The sixth letter in the third line ....
7. The seventh letter in the third line ....
8. The first letter in the second line ....
9. The sixth letter in the third line ....
10. The third letter in the second line ....
11. The third letter in the first line ....
12. The ninth letter in the second line ....
13. The first letter in the second line ....

Unit 2 WELCOME!

B Read this address list and then answer the questions.

| ADDRESS BOOK | | | 12:07pm |

Name	Address	Phone number	e-mail number
Brown, Penny	25, Victoria Road,		
	Oxford OX1 3WR	01865 641236	kan3@dial.pipex.com
Desmaris, Yves	17, rue Laforge,		
	Amiens, France	(00 33) 3 22 25 68 63	-
Green, Monica	9, Heathfield Street,		
	Liverpool L6 3BJ	0151 645 976	green@compuserve.com
Proctor, Chris	21 Beehive Lane,		
	Perth, W. Australia	(00 61) 9 5645 7685	chrisp@compuserve.com
Shaw, Christine	4, Fenton Road,		
	Redhill, Surrey		
	RH1 6RF	01373 657981	-
Schumacher, Ernst	Kaiser Wilhelm Ring 16,		
	Dusseldorf, Germany	(00 49) 211 45 65 78	eschumacher@weiss-mail.de

1. I'm the third person. What's my address? *9, Heathfield Street, Liverpool L6 3BJ*
2. I'm the second person. What's my telephone number?
3. I'm the fifth person. What's my postcode?
4. I'm the first person. What's my e-mail number?
5. I'm the sixth person. What's my family name?

7 Countries, cities and towns

Read these travel adverts and match
the countries with the cities and towns.

Countries	Cities and towns
Spain	Barcelona

Jet PLUS

▶▶▶ Discounted fares to all destinations ▶▶▶

Spain	£59	S Africa	£369
Portugal	£69	Canada	£149
Israel	£159	India	£299
Greece	£89	France	£82
Turkey	£89	Australia	£499
USA	£149	Germany	£96

Call 0171 359 6756

Lux Travel

Open 7 days. Flights from:

Athens	£169
Barcelona	£113
Berlin	£149
Calcutta	£310
Cape Town	£366
Denver	£220
Istanbul	£189
Lisbon	£96
Melbourne	£400
Montreal	£240
Paris	£109
Tel Aviv	£260

CAR HIRE CITY BREAKS
HOLIDAYS 0177 92777237

A Complete this form with *your* information.

NAME . . . .
ADDRESS . . . .
. . . . TOWN . . . .
POSTCODE . . . .
TEL (HOME) . . . .

The Danish Tourist Board, 55 Sloane Street, London SW1X 9SY

B Complete this form with a *friend's* information.

To World Journeys, FREEPOST GU4423 Petersfield, Hants GU33 1LP
Please send me details of your New Zealand Vineyard tours.

Name _____ **Address** _____

Postcode _____

Telephone _____

A ⊂⊃ Listen to the recording and answer the questions you hear.

B ⊂⊃ Listen again and write your answers here.

1. . . . .

2. . . . .

3. . . . .

4. . . . .

5. . . . .

⊂⊃ Where's the stress? Listen and choose the right word. □ = stress

1. hotel   hotel
2. address   address
3. welcome   welcome
4. reception   reception   reception
5. certainly   certainly   certainly

⊂⊃ Listen and repeat what you hear.

Complete the visual dictionary for Unit 2 on page 72.

Lost in time – EPISODE 2 ▢▢

The hot dog stand is near the park. It's not busy at two in the morning, but this morning a car is by the hot dog stand. A woman is in the car ...

JANA: *Excuse me, where's the hot dog stand?*
A MAN: *It's over there.*
JANA: *Oh, fine, thanks.*

A man with an ice cream, a woman, and an old woman are at the hot dog stand; a boy and girl are on the telephone at reception on the ground floor of a hotel. One or two men and women are in the restaurant.

JANA: *A hot dog, please.*
MAN: *One?*
JANA: *Yes, just one.*
MAN: *Here you are. The number 1 hot dogs in Prague!*
PIERRE: *Thanks a lot.*

In the park, an old man sings. Jana is near him.

JANA: *Mm, good old music.*

Pierre is at the hot dog stand, with his 'number 1' hot dog.
Suddenly, the car at the hot dog stand is near Pierre.

WOMAN: *Are you OK?*
PIERRE: *What?*
WOMAN: *I'm Olga. Look, your father is here ... your father, Pierre.*
PIERRE: *My dad's in Ireland.*

A moment later, Pierre is in the car with Olga and the man from the hot dog stand.

PIERRE: *Mum, mum ...Where's my mum?*
OLGA: *Is this the right boy?*
MAN: *Yes, it is. Quick. Go! Go!*

JANA: *Pierre! Pierre! This is terrible! Where's Pierre? Quick, the police!*
         Oh, please, the police! Where's my boy? My boy!

A man and woman are with Jana at the telephone in the hotel.

Pierre and the car are not in the city – they are on the road to an airport.
It's not the city airport. Where is it?

Unit 2 WELCOME!

PEOPLE AND THINGS IN MY LIFE

1 They're about 3

Complete the sentences under the pictures.
Use the words in the box.

| He | 40 | We | 60 | They |
| 3 | She | old | It | |

1. ..He..'s about 20.

3. ......'re ....

And you?

5. I'm ....

2. ....'s about ....

4. ....'re about ....

6. ....'s very ....

2 That's my business card

Complete the sentences with words from the box.

| my | his | her | our | their | business |
| girl | address book | letter | credit card | | |

1. That's ...our...
little ....

3. That's ....

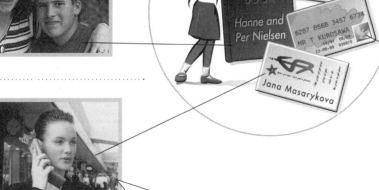

2. That's ....

4. That's m..... .... card.

5. That's ....

3 Yes, she is

A 📼 Listen and write the responses.

1. Is her husband OK? ....*Yes*......., ...*he*....... .....*is*...., he's fine.

2. Is her manager interesting? ...., ..., I think.

3. Are her colleagues nice? ...., ..., very nice.

4. Is this ring from Peru? ...., ..., from Lima.

5. She's his wife? ...., ... She's his second wife.

B Complete these sentences.

> **Questions and answers with *is/are***
>
> For questions with *Is he ...?* you answer *Yes/Yes,* .... *is* or *No/No, he isn't.*
>
> For questions with *Is she ...?* you answer *Yes/Yes,* .... or *No/No, she isn't.*
>
> For questions with *Are you ...?* you answer *Yes/Yes, I* .... or *No/No, I'm not.*
>
> For questions with *Are they ...?* you answer *Yes/Yes,* .... or *No/No, they aren't.*

4 Is that his wife?

📼 Listen and repeat the questions. Mark the two main stresses in question 5.

1. Is her hŭsband OK?

2. Is her mănager ĭnteresting?

3. Are her cŏlleagues nĭce?

4. Is this rĭng from Perŭ?

5. She's his wife?

5 Questionnaire

Answer the ten questions. Write:

Yes, I am; Yes, she is; Yes, he is; Yes, it is; Yes, they are
or
No, I'm not; No, she isn't; No, he isn't; No, it isn't; No, they aren't
or
I don't know.

Questions, questions, questions!

1 Is your car new?
....

2 Are you old?
....

3 Is your watch old?
....

4 Are business cards popular?
....

5 Is Spain popular?
....

6 Are mobile phones good?
....

7 Are you from Oslo?
....

8 Are earrings nice?
....

9 Is your bedroom interesting?
....

10 Are you busy?
....

Jana Masarykova

6 Thanks for the ...

🎧 Listen to the people and tick (✓) *thanks*, *thank you* or *thanks very much* under the correct picture.

	car	photograph	mobile phone	watch	ring	letter	phone book
thanks		✓					
thank you							
thanks very much							

7 My friend

Livia is my friend. She's from Slovakia. She's great.

Complete a description of your friend.

.... is .... friend. ....'s from ....

............'s ....

8 Number crossword

Complete the number crossword.

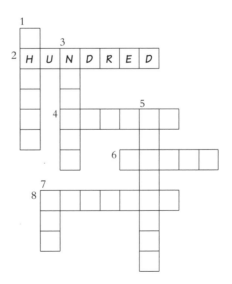

Across →
2. 110 − ten
4. 5 × sixteen
6. thirty × 2
8. 69 + one

Down ↓
1. six × 5
3. 70 + twenty
5. 10 + three
7. 66 ÷ eleven

Crossword: 2 Across: H U N D R E D

9 Visual dictionary

Complete the visual dictionary for Unit 3 on page 73.

Lost in time – EPISODE 3

It's night time. Pierre is at the airport with Olga and the man from the hot dog stand. The airport isn't a big one; the plane is not big. In the plane is a man.

Pierre is in the plane.

PIERRE: *Dad! Is it you?*
FATHER: *How are you, my boy? It's great to see you.*

Pierre is so pleased to be with his father.

PIERRE: *Is this your plane, Dad?*
FATHER: *Yes, Pierre, and it's your plane too.*
PIERRE: *What about Mum?*
FATHER: *Your mother and I are not … it's terrible for you, I know. Your mother is my third wife. We're … I'm not a very good husband … I'm a busy man, very busy. It isn't good, I know, but your mother she's … she's not nice to me. Look here's a letter from her.*

Pierre feels awful. His mother is wonderful, his father is wonderful, but his family is not wonderful. He is a boy – a boy with two parents – two parents and no home.
The plane is in the air.

PIERRE: *Where are we?*
FATHER: *We're near Ireland. Pierre, Ireland is your home.*

Pierre looks at his watch – it isn't a good day for a small boy.

Welcome to Ireland, says a man in the airport.

FATHER: *Thanks a lot, we're pleased to be here.*

Olga is there. A drink in the airport coffee shop and then they are in a car, a second car. It's a big car this time.

FATHER: *Bye, Pierre.*
PIERRE: *But Dad, where are you …?*
FATHER: *There's a big meeting, Pierre, in Dublin. I'm sorry. See you this evening, OK?*
PIERRE: *Mm … OK. Bye. But what about Mum?*
FATHER: *Bye.*

The big car is on a motorway. It's not very interesting for Pierre. They are at road exit number ten, but where is it? Where are they now?

Unit 3 PEOPLE AND THINGS IN MY LIFE

ABOUT TOWN

Fill the gaps in these questions with *is/are*, *a/an* or *any*. Then finish the answers to the questions with *is/isn't* or *are/aren't*.

1. ....*Is*.... there a nightclub in your town?   Yes, there ....

2. .... there any cathedrals in your country?   No, there ....

3. Are there .... people in the office?   Yes, there ....

4. Is there .... library in your town?   No, there ....

5. .... there .... opera house in your town?   Yes, there ....

6. .... there .... tourists in the hotel?   No, there ....

A Make up six questions about the picture. Start like this:

Is there a …?   *Are there any …?*

Write your questions here.

Example: *Are there any banks in the town?*

1. ....   4. ....

2. ....   5. ....

3. ....   6. ....

B Answer your six questions here.

Example: *Yes, there are two banks in the town.*

1. ....   4. ....

2. ....   5. ....

3. ....   6. ....

3 How old are they?

Look at the places in the photos. How old are they? Write a sentence for each place.
Use *over* and *about* in your sentences.

The Pompidou Centre, Paris, 1975

1. *The Pompidou Centre in Paris is over 20 years old.*

The Empire State Building, New York, 1931

2. ....

The New Shakespeare's Globe Theatre, London, 1997

3. ....

The Templo Sagrada Familia, Barcelona, 1882

4. ....

The Catholic Cathedral, Liverpool, 1967

5. ....
....

Tokyo City Hall, 1991

6. ....
....

4 Conversation

What does Sue say to Dave? Fill in the gaps in the conversation with one of the questions from the box.

> Where's this?   How old is it?
>   Really? That's very old.
> Really? That's very big.   Is it a big city?

DAVE: Here are my holiday photos.

SUE: Thanks. (1) *Where's this?* ....

DAVE: It's Rome.

SUE: (2) ....

DAVE: Yes, it is. There are over three million people.

SUE: (3) ....

DAVE: And that's the Colosseum.

SUE: (4) ....

DAVE: I think it's about two thousand years old.

SUE: (5) ....

Unit 4 ABOUT TOWN

5 North, south, east, west

A Write sentences about the Australian cities on the map.
Use the words *north*, *south*, *east* and *west*.

Example: *Newcastle is in the east of Australia.*

1. Melbourne ....

2. Perth ....

3. Darwin ....

4. Brisbane ....

B Write about four cities or towns in your country. (Don't write about the capital city of your country.)

1. .... is in the north of my country.

2. ....

3. ....

4. ....

6 Puzzles

A Read the clues and make words. Follow the example.
This is a country.

Example:

U	N	I	V	E	R	S	I	T	Y

1. a place for students over 18

2. a place for sports: sports ....

3. new, not old

4. a place for police, buses and trains

5. 1,000,000 = one ....

6. a lot of books are here

7. 100 = one ....

8. 1,000 = one ....

B Write the numbers. Follow the example.

Example: rhitty-wot × rfuo = ...*a hundred and twenty-eight*....

1. nextise × neetvense = ...

2. yttnew-noe × runtefoe = ...

3. higyet-ienn × eeennnti = ...

4. tiffy-vief × tixys-xis = ...

5. tow handouts x neleev = ...

7 Washington

Read about Washington. Fill the gaps with words from the box.

| capital | city | country | east | famous | parks | people |

Washington is the (1) .... *capital* .... of the USA. It is in the (2) ....

of the (3) .... It is a big (4) .... with about three million

(5) .... The Capitol and the White House are in Washington. There is also

a (6) .... library, the Library of Congress, and there are a lot of lovely

(7) ....

8 My country

Fill in this box about the capital city of your country.

My capital city
Country: ....
City: ....
Where: .... (north, south, east, west)
Number of people: ....
Famous: ....

9 Join in the conversation

A ⊞ Listen to the conversation and answer the questions.

B ⊞ Listen again and write your answers here.

....

....

....

....

....

10 Sounds

A Which word sounds different? Underline one word.

1. <u>age</u> thank am bad

2. two you do house

3. are bank map thanks

4. his city think like

5. sell key get west

⊞ Listen to the recording. Is your answer right?

B Where's the stress? Choose the right word.

1. famous □̇   famous □̇
2. museum □̇   museum □̇   museum □̇
3. festival □̇   festival □̇   festival □̇
4. cathedral □̇   cathedral □̇   cathedral □̇
5. important □̇   important □̇   important □̇

 Listen to the recording. Check your answers.

Complete the visual dictionary for Unit 4 on page 74.

Lost in time – EPISODE 4

Olga and Pierre are in a small town with a school, a sports centre, a theatre and a tourist information office. It's an old town – the church is old and there's an old castle with a museum. Olga and Pierre are now in the post office.

OLGA: *Excuse me, where's Skilogallee House?*
WOMAN: *It's about two kilometres north of here.*
MAN: *Yes, here's Skilogallee House on this map.*
OLGA: *Thanks for your help.*

Skilogallee House is wonderful. It's about 500 years old with very small windows. On the ground floor is the kitchen, a very big living room with old pictures of important Irish men and women and maps of the town, a room with a television and two computers and an office with phones, letters, books and a lamp. On the first floor are the bedrooms and bathroom. There's a library on the second floor but the door is locked.

OLGA: *This is your room, Pierre.*
PIERRE: *Is there a phone number for my mother?*
OLGA: *Ask your father this evening.*

Pierre looks at the books in the office. There is a book called *The family in modern European cinema*. Interesting! In the book is a photo of Prague ... near the hotel and the hot dog stand. Is his mother in the photo? No, she isn't.
It is evening. His father is in the house. The phone rings. His father answers.

FATHER: *Jana? No, she's not here. I'm sorry, she's with her mother in Prague.*

Pierre is in the living room. Is it a man or woman on the phone? Is it his mother?
Pierre is suddenly near the phone.

PIERRE: *Mum, Mum, where are you?*
FATHER: *It's not your mother, Pierre, sssh. Sorry about that. OK. Yes, that's fine. Thank you. Bye.*

Pierre's father looks at him.

FATHER: *Hey, Pierre, how about this? Write a letter to your mother this evening and take the letter to the post office in the morning.*
PIERRE: *Yes, please.*

Pierre is in his room with his second letter. The first letter is terrible and is on the floor. But the second letter is OK for a young boy, a young boy with no home. In the letter is his telephone number.

I'VE GOT ONE ON THE WALL

1 He's got a sister

Complete the sentences.

4. They've .... a big
   f............................ .

You?

1. He's got a ....*sister*.....

2. He's .... a ....
   and a ....

3. .... got a
   h........................ .

5. I've got ....

2 Clocks at home?

Write *some* or *any* in the spaces.

Have you got (1) .....*any*..... clocks in your home?

Really? We've got (2) ....

Mm. We've got a clock in the kitchen, one in the living room and one in the bathroom.

No, we haven't got (4) .... in our bedroom.

Where?

No.

Have you?

(3) .... in the bedroom?

My sister's got (5) .... clocks in the toilet!

Listen and check your answers.

3 A red letter day

Label the colours of the things in the picture.

| green red blue white yellow |

4 Mini conversations

Write one word from box A and one word from box B in the spaces in the conversations.

1 I'm .... tired ....

Go to .... then.

2 I've got a ....

Have you? Take some ....

3 Good ....

Good night. See you in the
....

Box A

| night   tired   headache |

Box B

| tablets   morning   bed |

📼 Listen and check your answers.

○○ Read the information about flat 1 and flat 2. Listen to the two conversations. Two things are not correct in each. Correct the information.

Flat 1: Mile End
Three bedrooms
New bathroom and kitchen
£215 a week

Flat 2: Hendon
Two bedrooms
New kitchen
No TV
£175 a week

A Read the adverts for accommodation. Match the accommodation with the correct place and the price.

KENSINGTON GARDENS

Nice person (20–30) with job to share 3-bedroomed house with professional man and woman; $60 per week. Call Peta 8247 3320.

West Lakes

New flat $230 p.w. lakefront
3 bedrooms, lounge, kitchen, carport, no pets.
8246 5581

Enfield

Room with bed, chairs, TV, fridge; share kitchen and bathroom; near shops and train station, suit student, $50 per week.

8593 2246.

Place	Accommodation	Price
West Lakes	Room	$60
Kensington Gardens	Flat	$50
Enfield	House	$230

B Answer these questions.

1. Is the flat in West Lakes old? Yes/No
2. Has the room in Enfield got any furniture? Yes/No
3. Is it a house in Kensington Gardens? Yes/No
4. Is the flat in West Lakes OK for my cat? Yes/No

7 Your accommodation advert

Write an advert in English for your house or flat or room for a tourist magazine.

Remember!

Place
Accommodation:
– rooms
– nice things about the accommodation
Price per week

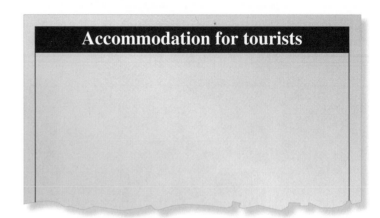

Accommodation for tourists

8 Ask the person on the plane

You are on a plane. Ask the woman 6 questions. Start your questions with *Have you got …/Has your …* and complete the questions with expressions from boxes A and B. (Remember! *any a*)

A

ClAir

| CHILDREN | DOG | PEN, PLEASE |
| PRESENTS | MAGAZINE | DOLLARS |

Examples: *Have you got **a** business card?*
*Have you got **any** water?*
*Have you got **any** books?*

1. ....
2. ....
3. ....

B

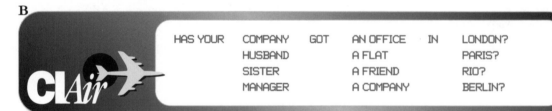

ClAir

HAS YOUR	COMPANY	GOT	AN OFFICE	IN	LONDON?
	HUSBAND		A FLAT		PARIS?
	SISTER		A FRIEND		RIO?
	MANAGER		A COMPANY		BERLIN?

Example: *Has your sister got a flat in Rio?*

4. ....
5. ....
6. ....

9 Visual dictionary

Complete the visual dictionary for Unit 5 on page 75.

Lost in time – EPISODE 5 ◘◘

'Come on, Pierre,' Olga says from the window of the car, 'and don't forget your sunglasses, it's a beautiful day.' Pierre has got his letter but not his sunglasses.

It's five minutes to the town from Skilogallee House in the car, ten minutes by bus (when there is one!) and 30 minutes by horse and cart. There are one or two holiday homes on the road into town and a small hotel with beautiful little windows.

In the post office, Pierre posts the letter to his mother. He listens – the letter box is empty. That's fine. So his letter is special – the only one for Prague.

Olga is in a shop called Travelworld. Pierre is by the open door of the shop. He listens to bits of the conversation.
'... fly to Singapore, then to ... no, don't go to Tokyo ... here, have a look at this. Yes. On Thursday the ninth from Dublin? Yes, here are the tickets.'

They are in the car again. 'What are the tickets for?' Pierre asks.
'Don't ask now. Wait till we get home,' Olga answers.
'Home! That's a stupid word,' Pierre says.
'OK, OK, Skilogallee House,' says Olga.
'No, tell me about the tickets now!' says Pierre.
'No, Pierre, later.'
'No, now, NOW!' says Pierre.

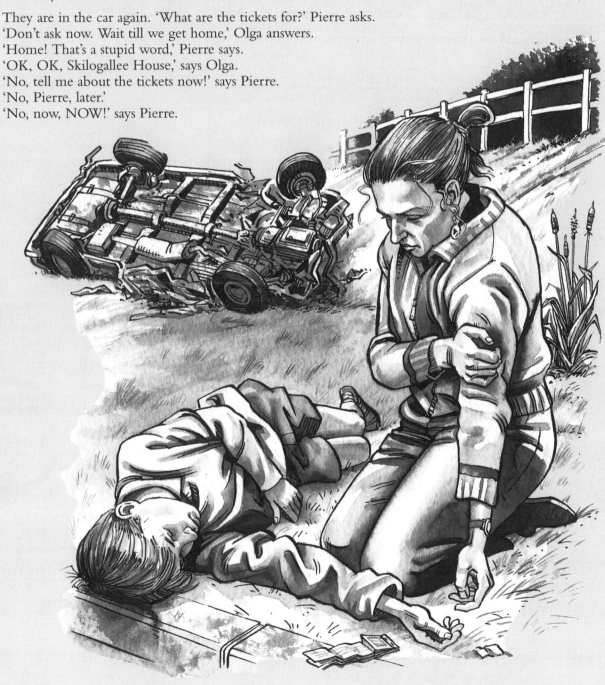

A minute later the car is upside down in a ditch by the road. Olga is OK, but Pierre is not OK. He is by the road. The tickets – tickets to New Zealand – are in the road too. It is Tuesday the 7th of May.

DON'T FORGET YOUR SUNGLASSES

---

1 Countries, cities, descriptions

Think of countries that you know. List cities you know in the countries. Choose a
description from the box for each city.

beautiful   lovely   wonderful   cheap   modern   interesting

dirty   awful   expensive   busy   terrible

	Country	City	Description
Examples:	Australia	Sydney	beautiful, modern
	Indonesia	Jakarta	interesting, busy
1.	....	....	....
2.	....	....	....
3.	....	....	....
4.	....	....	....

---

2 Go? Don't go?

Write the opposites of the sentences.

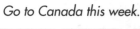

Go to Canada this week.

No, don't go to Canada this week.

Example:

1. Don't go to Hungary this November.

   Yes, ...

2. Take your camera on the tour.

   No, ...

3. Don't stay at the Premier Hotel.

   Yes, ...

4. Tell the travel agent about the hotel bedroom.

   No, ...

5. Phone the tourist information office.

   No, ...

Read the questions, then find the answers in the text.

1. Which heading is not in the text?
   – Buses
   – Travelling at night
   – Travel times
   – Travelcards
   – Travelling in London
   – The Underground

2. For how many hours is the Underground open every day?

3. Is 11.30 a busy time on the Underground on Monday? Yes/No

4. Are Compulsory and Request stops the same? Yes/No

5. Are there Night Buses at 00.20? Yes/No

6. Are there maps at the London Travel Information Centres? Yes/No

Travelling in London

Welcome to London, a city with much to offer the business traveller or tourist. Travelling in London is easy. Use buses or the Underground. Plan your journeys with the help of this information.

The Underground
This is open for 20 hours every day. Buy your tickets from the ticket office or ticket machines at any Underground station. Don't travel at the busy times 08.00–09.30 and 17.00–18.30 Mondays to Fridays.

Buses
There are 17,000 bus stops in London, and two types of bus stop:

  Compulsory – Buses stop (but not when full)

  Request – Put out your hand to stop the bus.

Travelling at night
After about 00.30, use our many Night Buses. They pass through Trafalgar Square and go to many hotels.

Travelcards
There are one-day travelcards, weekend travelcards, family travelcards and weekly travelcards. Call at a London Travel Information Centre for maps and information.

4 My city on the Internet

Complete this text about your city or town as part of an Internet reply to a person in South Africa.

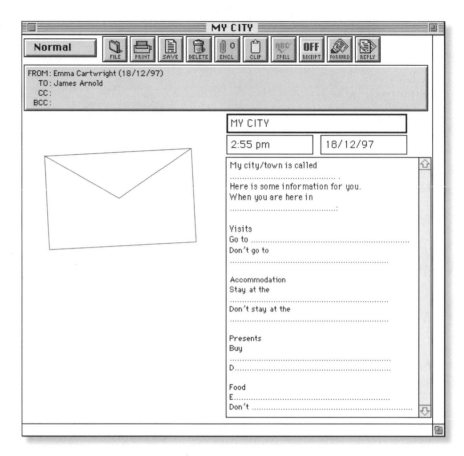

FROM: Emma Cartwright (18/12/97)
TO : James Arnold
CC :
BCC :

MY CITY

2:55 pm   18/12/97

My city/town is called
....
Here is some information for you.
When you are here in
.... :

Visits
Go to ....
Don't go to
....

Accommodation
Stay at the
....
Don't stay at the
....

Presents
Buy
....
D..

Food
E..
Don't ....

5 Where are my sunglasses?

Look at the picture. Answer the questions.

1. Where are my sunglasses? They're *by the suitcase* ....

2. What about my camera? It's ....

3. Good. Is my passport there? Yes, ...

4. And my CDs? ....
   OK. Thanks.

⊂⊃ Listen and check.

6 Days of the week

Look at this diary for the week. Listen and answer the questions. Say the correct day.

Monday	meeting
Tuesday	conference cinema
Wednesday	restaurant
Thursday	police station library
Friday	disco
Saturday	sports centre
Sunday	university

7 Visual dictionary

Complete the visual dictionary for Unit 6 on page 76.

Lost in time – EPISODE 6

The hospital is new with orange walls. Pierre's room is orange and white.
Pierre is in a bed – his eyes are closed. His father is with him.

'I'm so sorry, Pierre. Look, I've got some pictures for you. I've got a picture of your mother and you on your birthday with a birthday present – that little blue clock for your bedroom wall, from your aunt, look!'

A doctor comes in. Pierre's father starts a question, 'When is Pierre ...?'
The doctor knows the question and answers, 'I'm sorry, but it's hard to say – tomorrow, a year, two years – we don't know, but Pierre is in good hands here. Come back later. We've got one or two things to look at now, I'm afraid. Go home, take some tablets, go to bed.'
The curtains are round the bed.

Pierre's father sits down on a sofa in Skilogallee House. He looks old, old and tired.
He looks at the phone.

Is it important to phone Pierre's mother? No, it's not the right thing. Forget it!
He asks Olga about Pierre's mother.
'No,' she says, 'it's not a good thing to talk to his mother about this. When Pierre is OK,
phone then.'
'What about the tickets to New Zealand?' asks Olga.
'Forget New Zealand,' answers Pierre's father, 'I've got a son, a son in hospital, in a coma.
When he's OK, it's OK to talk about New Zealand, but not today.'

Unit 6 DON'T FORGET YOUR SUNGLASSES

7

TIME FOR WORK

1 Differences

Fill in the gaps with the correct forms of the verbs.

Example: *I live in France. My brother **doesn't live in France.***
He ...lives... in Switzerland.

1. I work in an office. My sister ....

   She .... in a shop.

2. My father gets up very early. I ....

   I .... late.

3. I have breakfast at 6 o'clock. My brother ....

   He .... at 7 o'clock.

4. My friend finishes work at 11 o'clock at night. I ....

   I .... 6 o'clock in the evening.

5. I watch television every evening. My sister ....

   She .... at the weekend.

2 People and their work

A Read about three people and their jobs.

	1	2	3
Name	John	Mandi	Elaine
Job	travel agent	journalist	teacher
Place	shop in London	office and sports centres in Dublin	English school in Egypt
Start	9.00 a.m.	1.00 p.m.	8.30 a.m.
Finish	6.00 p.m.	11.00 p.m.	4.15 p.m.
Work	serve customers	watch sports interview people write about sport	teach children 4–5 years old

B You want to interview three people about their jobs.
Finish these interview questions.

1. NAME   What's *your name* .... ?

2. JOB   What .... ?

3. PLACE   Where .... ?

4. START   When .... ?

5. FINISH   What time .... ?

6. DO (work)   What do you .... (in your office)?

C Write John's and Mandi's answers to your six questions.

	John	Mandi
1.	*My name's John.*	....
2.	....	*I'm a journalist.*
3.	....	....
4.	....	....
5.	....	....
6.	....	....

D Now write six sentences about Elaine. Start like this:

Her name is Elaine. She is a teacher. ....

....

....

....

....

....

....

---

3 Questions to answers

Here are some answers. What were the questions?

	Answer	*Question*
Example:	I work in an office.	*Where do you work?*
1.	He works in a department store.	.... ?
2.	She's a doctor.	.... ?
3.	I get up at 6 o'clock.	.... ?
4.	No, she doesn't. She works in New York.	.... in Washington?
5.	They live in Moscow.	.... ?
6.	He finishes work at 6 o'clock.	.... ?

A Write numbers from the box next to the right words.

| 20.20 | 09.15 | ~~14.10~~ | 23.55 | 11.25 | 02.30 | 16.40 | 13.45 |
| 19.05 | 07.35 | | | | | | |

1. ten past two in the afternoon .... 14.10 ....

2. half past two in the morning ....

3. twenty-five past eleven in the morning ....

4. a quarter to two in the afternoon ....

5. a quarter past nine in the morning ....

6. five to twelve at night ....

7. twenty past eight in the evening ....

8. five past seven in the evening ....

9. twenty to five in the afternoon ....

10. twenty-five to eight in the morning ....

B Draw the times on the clocks.

twenty-five past six   ten to eleven   one o'clock   a quarter past seven   half past two

A Match a job and an action with an ending.

Jobs	Actions	Ending
1. teacher	serve	people in hospital
2. doctor	write	customers in a café
3. waiter	have	in a newspaper
4. scientist	help	in a laboratory
5. businessperson	teach	school or university
6. journalist	work	meetings in an office

B Now write sentences like this:

1. ... A teacher teaches in a school or university. ....

2. ....

3. ....

4. ....

5. ....

6. ....

Fill the gaps with one of the words from the box.

at	for	from	in	of	to	with

My name's Ed Stanbury. I'm the manager (1) ....*of*...... a big department store (2) ....

London. I get up (3) .... 6.30 and I start work (4) .... 8.30. Sometimes I go

(5) .... other cities and have meetings (6) .... other shop managers. We have over

a hundred shop assistants in the London store. They talk (7) .... customers and sell

things (8) .... them. Customers buy cheap things and expensive things (9) .... our

shops. I have an office and a secretary. My secretary writes letters (10) .... me.

A Find ten people. (There are five jobs, two people in families and three other words for people.) Words can go up (↑), down (↓), forwards (→), backwards (←), or diagonally (↘).

```
E  D  O  C  T  O  R  W
M  N  F  B  O  S  S  A
N  O  G  R  S  S  W  I
U  N  T  I  I  R  P  T
R  A  O  H  N  E  Y  E
S  M  N  L  E  E  N  R
E  E  F  I  W  R  E  D
L  A  W  Y  E  R  O  R
```

B Take a word from box A and a word from box B and make two-word nouns. There are some clues to help you.

Box A

department	football	living	primary	shop	travel	university

Box B

agent	assistant	room	school	stadium	store	student

Example: *A school for young children.* ...*primary school*...............

1. He or she works in a shop. ....

2. He or she helps you to go from place to place. ....

3. A learner over 18. ....

4. A very big shop. ....

5. A place in a house. ....

6. Go here to see sport. ....

A Read this travel plan and answer the questions.

1. Who is the travel agent?
2. Who is the customer?

NEW Intertravel **LTD**

For: Mr P Jarvis
OUT
TRAVEL DATE   Thur. 14 DEC Flight No. BA 680
CHECK IN   14.40   Heathrow Airport
DEPART   15.55   London Heathrow
ARRIVE   21.45   Istanbul

RETURN
TRAVEL DATE   Sat. 16 DEC Flight No. BA 675
CHECK IN   07.45   Atatürk Airport
DEPART   08.45   Istanbul
ARRIVE   11.00   London Heathrow

ITINERARY ... ITINERARY ... ITINERARY ... I

B You are the customer. Answer these questions.

1. When do you check in at Heathrow Airport?
   I check in at twenty to three in the afternoon.

2. When does your flight go from Heathrow?

3. When do you get to Istanbul?

4. What day do you come back from Turkey?

5. What time do you check in at Istanbul?

6. When do you get back to London?

9 Join in the conversation

A 🔲 Listen to the recording and answer the questions you hear.

B 🔲 Listen again and write your answers here.

10 Visual dictionary

Complete the visual dictionary for Unit 7 on pages 77–78.

Lost in time – EPISODE 7 ▣

'What time is it?' asks Pierre's father.
'Two thirty,' answers the nurse.
'Is Pierre ...?'
'No, he's the same,' she says. 'I'm sorry.'
'That's OK,' says Pierre's father.
They sit near Pierre's bed and talk.
'What do you do?' asks the nurse.
'I have a clothes company, an international clothes company,' says Pierre's father.
'Sounds interesting. You look very tired. Is it a busy job?' she asks.
'Yes. There's a lot of travel, hours on the mobile phone, meetings,' says Pierre's father.
'Do you see your doctor very often?' she asks.
'No, there's no time for doctors,' answers Pierre's father.
'You don't look so good, do you want to see a doctor here?' asks the nurse.
'No, I'm fine, really,' says Pierre's father.

They look at Pierre.

'He's a nice boy. How old is he?' asks the nurse.
'He's eight, no, he's nine on Friday.'
'It's his birthday on Friday? Then how about a birthday party and some presents?'
'No, it's OK.'
'Come on,' says the nurse. 'I think it helps sometimes. Pierre is asleep, but perhaps he listens in his head. A party for Pierre is a great idea!'
'Oh, OK,' says Pierre's father.

Unit 7 TIME FOR WORK

A Read this travel plan and answer the questions.

1. Who is the travel agent?
2. Who is the customer?

NEW Intertravel **LTD**

ITINERARY ... ITINERARY ... ITINERARY ... I

For: Mr P Jarvis
OUT

TRAVEL DATE		Thur. 14 DEC Flight No. BA 680
CHECK IN	14.40	Heathrow Airport
DEPART	15.55	London Heathrow
ARRIVE	21.45	Istanbul

RETURN

TRAVEL DATE		Sat. 16 DEC Flight No. BA 675
CHECK IN	07.45	Atatürk Airport
DEPART	08.45	Istanbul
ARRIVE	11.00	London Heathrow

B You are the customer. Answer these questions.

1. When do you check in at Heathrow Airport?
   I check in at twenty to three in the afternoon.

2. When does your flight go from Heathrow?

3. When do you get to Istanbul?

4. What day do you come back from Turkey?

5. What time do you check in at Istanbul?

6. When do you get back to London?

9 Join in the conversation

listening and speaking

A ☐☐ Listen to the recording and answer the questions you hear.

B ☐☐ Listen again and write your answers here.

10 Visual dictionary

Complete the visual dictionary for Unit 7 on pages 77–78.

Lost in time – EPISODE 7 ◧

'What time is it?' asks Pierre's father.
'Two thirty,' answers the nurse.
'Is Pierre ...?'
'No, he's the same,' she says. 'I'm sorry.'
'That's OK,' says Pierre's father.
They sit near Pierre's bed and talk.
'What do you do?' asks the nurse.
'I have a clothes company, an international clothes company,' says Pierre's father.
'Sounds interesting. You look very tired. Is it a busy job?' she asks.
'Yes. There's a lot of travel, hours on the mobile phone, meetings,' says Pierre's father.
'Do you see your doctor very often?' she asks.
'No, there's no time for doctors,' answers Pierre's father.
'You don't look so good, do you want to see a doctor here?' asks the nurse.
'No, I'm fine, really,' says Pierre's father.

They look at Pierre.

'He's a nice boy. How old is he?' asks the nurse.
'He's eight, no, he's nine on Friday.'
'It's his birthday on Friday? Then how about a birthday party and some presents?'
'No, it's OK.'
'Come on,' says the nurse. 'I think it helps sometimes. Pierre is asleep, but perhaps he listens in his head. A party for Pierre is a great idea!'
'Oh, OK,' says Pierre's father.

Unit 7 TIME FOR WORK

Pierre's father has his head in his hands.

'What's the matter? asks the nurse.

'It's just a headache, I think. I'm OK,' answers Pierre's father.

'Are you sure?' she asks.

'Yes,' says Pierre's father, 'I've got some tablets.'

'I have a journalist friend,' says the nurse. 'Pierre's birthday is a great story. Do you think I ...'

'No, no, no journalists,' says Pierre's father. 'This is a family thing.'

'What about Pierre's mother?' she asks.

'Oh, er, she's not in Ireland at the moment. She lives in the Czech Republic.'

'Does she know about Pierre?'

'Er ... I don't know her address. What time is it now?'

'Erm, it's three fifteen.'

'Three fifteen? Look, I've got a plane to get at six in the city. I'm sorry.'

'That's OK,' says the nurse. 'Call a taxi from my office. Don't forget to come again on Friday for Pierre's party.'

'Yes, of course, and thank you.'

'Don't mention it.'

'See you.'

'Bye.'

Pierre's father is not OK; his headache is bad, but he hasn't got time for a doctor.

INTERNATIONAL FOOD

Complete these sentences with *like/likes* or *love/loves* + type of food.

Example: I ..*like*.. ..*Greek*.. food.

1. I .... food.

2. My friend .... food.

3. My brother (sister) .... food.

4. My parents .... food.

5. My ....

> I like Indian food.

> Do you?

> Mm, it's great.

A Complete the responses to the questions in these mini conversations.

1	2	3
I like Indian food.	Do you?	Mm, it's great.
I don't like English food.	Don't you?	No, it's not very nice.
My mother likes Thai food.	...........................?	Yes, she eats it a lot.
They love sandwiches.	...........................?	Mm, very much.
My fish likes bread.	...........................?	Yes, it eats a lot of bread.
We don't like black coffee.	.... you?	No, it's very strong.
My brother likes rice.	...........................?	Yes, he loves it.

⊂⊃ Listen and check your answers.

B ⊂⊃ Listen again and say part 2.

3 Airline menu

Read this menu from an airline. Are the sentences
true or false?

1. There is coffee and tea with supper and with breakfast. T/F
2. There is fish but not meat for supper. T/F
3. The plane doesn't go to Singapore. T/F
4. There is fruit for supper and for breakfast. T/F
5. Salad is the first thing for breakfast. T/F

SUPPER

SEASONAL SALAD
CHICKEN WITH TOMATO AND BASIL
OR
PERCH FISH WITH SATAY PEANUT SAUCE
MANDARIN YOGHURT GATEAU
COFFEE   TEA

BREAKFAST

APPLE JUICE
WARM FRUIT MUFFIN
COFFEE   TEA

ClAir
FLIGHT C1200 THAILAND TO MEXICO

4 Letter from a student in another country

Complete this letter. Write *and* or *but* in the spaces.

The family are OK. I like the mother (1) .... father (2) .... I don't like their
son, Jordi – he's terrible. His sister, Elizabeth, is nice (3) .... little Eva is awful
– she talks all the time! Their friends are great – some of their friends, that is!
Johann (4) .... Christian are fantastic, (5) .... Frans isn't so nice.
It's not easy to write this. I don't like the food in this home (6) .... I don't like
the city.
This is my last letter to you. I'm off to Singapore. I've got a new job (7) ....
I'm very happy. Thanks for your phone call (8) .... for your letter!

Lars

PS Please write!

5 Where's my new bag?

Put the correct beginning with the correct ending and make good questions.

Beginning
1. How many days ...
2. What's your ...
3. Where's my new ...
4. How ...
5. How long is ...
6. When ...

Ending
a. ... are you?
b. ... are there in July?
c. ... first name?
d. ... bag?
e. ... is your birthday?
f. ... your English course?

6 Asking and answering

A ▭ Listen and repeat the questions.

B ▭ Listen again and answer the questions.

7 I love fish

▭ Listen to the conversation in the restaurant. Tick (✓) the food they like and cross
(✗) the food they don't like.

Paul (He): fish   Thai curry   Indian curry   Indian bread   rice

Daniella (She): fish   Thai food   Indian food   Indian bread   rice

8 Visual dictionary

Complete the visual dictionary for Unit 8 on page 79.

Lost in time – EPISODE 8 ⚋

It is August – five years later.

It is Pierre's fifth birthday in hospital. Five years of sleep; five years of silence. This year Pierre's father is not at the hospital. There is a table with food on it: sandwiches (chicken, cheese), 14 candles in a big cake, a big bottle of Coca-cola.

The nurses sing 'Happy Birthday' and look at Pierre, but there is no answer, no smile on his mouth, nothing.

FIRST NURSE:	*I like these sandwiches.*
SECOND NURSE:	*Mm. Good, aren't they?*
FIRST NURSE:	*The other children here always like the cake too.*
SECOND NURSE:	*So do I!*
FIRST NURSE:	*(cuts the cake) OK, here you are! Happy birthday, Pierre!*
SECOND NURSE:	*But how many more birthdays for Pierre in this room?*
FIRST NURSE:	*I've no idea, but it's no life for a boy.*
SECOND NURSE:	*He's not a boy now, really, he's a young man.*

The two nurses talk near the table of food. They talk about husbands, children, work – the usual things. There is a noise. They stop talking.

SECOND NURSE:	*What's that?*
FIRST NURSE:	*What's what?*
SECOND NURSE:	*That noise.*
FIRST NURSE:	*Nothing – just you, and the cake!*

They talk again, about food and restaurants: French, Thai and the new Mexican restaurant near the hospital.

The noise again.

FIRST NURSE:	*What's that?*

MONEY! MONEY! MONEY!

A This family wants to sell some of their old things. Fill the spaces with the correct words from the box.

bed	books	CDs	fridge	lamp	magazines	painting	radio
suitcase	umbrella	camera	clock				

a ....
b ....
c ....
d ....
e ....
f ....
g ....
h ....
i ....
j ....
k ....
l ....

B Make up questions for ten of the things in the picture.

Examples: *bed/books cost*   How much does/do the bed/books cost?
              bed/books be   How much is/are the bed/books?

1. bed cost ....
2. books be ....
3. CDs cost ....
4. fridge cost ....
5. lamp be ....
6. magazines be ....
7. painting cost ....
8. radio be ....
9. suitcase be ....
10. umbrella cost ....

C Answer the ten questions like this.

It/they costs/cost thirty dollars.
It is/they are one dollar each or five dollars for ten.

1. ....

2. ....

3. ....

4. ....

5. ....

6. ....

7. ....

8. ....

9. ....

10. ....

---

2 Shopping

You are in a shop. You want to buy three things. Write your part of the conversations.
Use this language.

Have you got ..., please?
Can I have ..., please?
I'd like ..., please.
How much ...?

1. You want to buy a T-shirt.

    ASSISTANT: Hello, can I help you?

    YOU:　　　 (T-shirt) I'd like (1) ...... *a T-shirt, please.* ....

    ASSISTANT: What colour would you like?

    YOU:　　　 (green?) (2) ....

    ASSISTANT: Yes, we have. What size would you like? Large or small?

    YOU:　　　 (large) (3) ....

    ASSISTANT: Here you are.

    YOU:　　　 (Ask the price.) (4) ....

2. You want to buy some shoes.

    YOU:　　　 (shoes) I'd (1) ....

    ASSISTANT: What size are you?

    YOU:　　　 (38 or 44) (2) ....

    ASSISTANT: What colour would you like?

    YOU:　　　 (brown?) (3) ....

    ASSISTANT: No, we haven't. We've got blue or black.

    YOU:　　　 (blue) (4) ....

    ASSISTANT: Here you are.

    YOU:　　　 (Ask the price.) (5) ....

    ASSISTANT: They're twenty dollars.

    YOU:　　　 (cheap) (6) ....

---

3. You want to buy an umbrella.

ASSISTANT: Good morning. Can I help you?

YOU: (umbrella) Yes, I'd (1) ....

ASSISTANT: Yes, of course. What colour would you like?

YOU: (black?) (2) ....

ASSISTANT: Yes, we have. What size?

YOU: (small) (3) ....

ASSISTANT: We've got two small black umbrellas. Here they are.

YOU: (Ask the price.) (4) ....

ASSISTANT: The small one is thirty pounds and the very small one is forty pounds.

YOU: (Say that's very expensive. Buy the small umbrella.) (5) ....

....

ASSISTANT: Yes, of course.

3 Questions and answers

A Start these six questions with the correct question words from this box.

when	what	who	where	how

	Questions	Answers
1.	**What** .... colour would you like?	**Green and blue.** ....
2.	.... much is this car?	....
3.	.... is your credit card number?	....
4.	.... are you from?	....
5.	.... is this T-shirt for?	....
6.	.... do you want to pay?	....

B Now find the best short answers to questions 1–6 and write them under *Answers*.

a. My brother.
b. By credit card.
c. Five four three four, six one two nine, seven seven five one, five eight two four.
d. Three thousand pounds.
e. Australia.
f. Green and blue.

4 Word lists

Add five words from the box to each of the three lists on the next page.

actress	assistant	boyfriend	children	credit card	dollar	eat
freezer	fridge	grandson	lunch	pay	price	snack	wallet

	Money	*Food*	*People*
Examples:	cost	breakfast	father
	....	....	....
	....	....	....
	....	....	....
	....	....	....

5 Word puzzle

Fill in the words. One word is in the puzzle already.

Across

1. Not expensive
2. Spanish money
3. Place to keep money
4. Small meal
5. My earrings are .... not gold.
6. Small children play with these things.
7. Place to keep food cold
8. £3 = three ....
9. Earrings, ring and necklace are three kinds of ....

Down

10. A book of things to buy

4. S N A C K

6 Choose some shoes

A Look at these shoes from a sports catalogue. Which ones do you like best? How much do they cost?

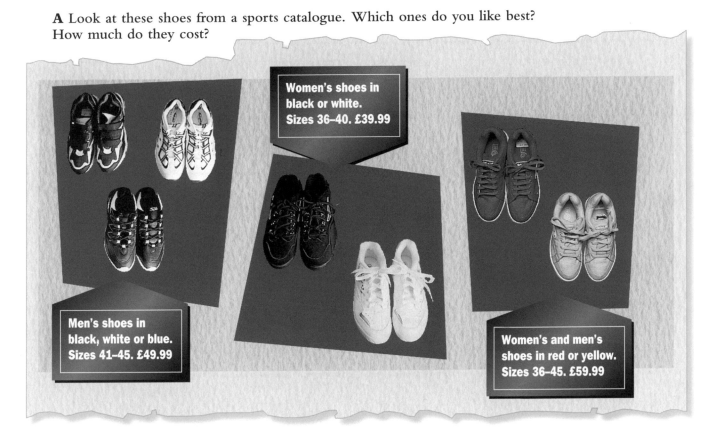

Women's shoes in black or white.
Sizes 36–40. £39.99

Men's shoes in black, white or blue.
Sizes 41–45. £49.99

Women's and men's shoes in red or yellow.
Sizes 36–45. £59.99

B Answer these questions.

1. Have they got what these people want? Answer *Yes* or *No*.

   a. I'm a woman. I want some black shoes. I'm size 36. ....

   b. I'm a man. I want some red shoes. I'm size 37. ....

   c. I'm a woman. I want some blue shoes. I'm size 37. ....

   d. I'm a man. I want some white shoes. I'm size 42. ....

   e. I want some yellow shoes for my brother. He's size 43. ....

   f. I want some black shoes for my sister. She's size 33. ....

2. How much are these shoes?

   a. Red shoes for women ....

   b. Black shoes for men ....

   c. Yellow shoes for women ....

   d. White shoes for men ....

   e. Black shoes for women ....

7 Mail order

Order four pairs of shoes: one for yourself, one for a friend and two for people in your family. Fill in the form.

Home Address

MR/MS/MRS/MISS

ADDRESS

POSTCODE

TELEPHONE

PRODUCT NAME	CODE	1ST CHOICE COLOUR	2ND CHOICE COLOUR	SIZE	TOTAL £	P

	Total price of items	
	Standard post & packing	
	TOTAL	

☐ **Cheque**
Please include your address and cheque card number on the back

☐ **Mastercard**

☐ **American Express**

☐ **Visa**

☐ **Delta/Connect**

Please quote card number and expiry date

☐☐☐☐ ☐☐☐☐ ☐☐☐☐ ☐☐☐☐

Expiry date ☐ ☐ ☐ ☐

Cardholder's signature

8 Prices on the phone

A 🔲 Listen to a telephone conversation. Write the prices.

Thing	Price	Catalogue number
1. Computer disks	....	....
2. Casio calculator	....	....
3. Desk chair	....	....
4. Box of black pens (50)	....	....
TOTAL	....	

B 🔲 Listen again and write in the catalogue numbers.

9 Visual dictionary

Complete the visual dictionary for Unit 9 on page 80.

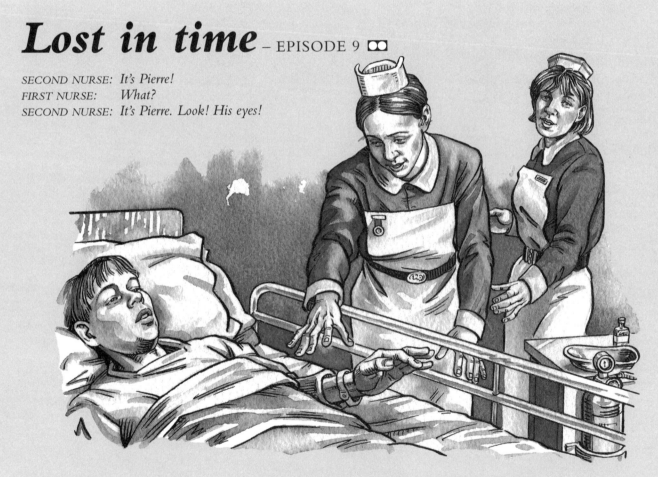

Lost in time – EPISODE 9 🔲

SECOND NURSE: *It's Pierre!*
FIRST NURSE: *What?*
SECOND NURSE: *It's Pierre. Look! His eyes!*

Pierre's eyes are open! The noise is from his hand on the bed. The two nurses are excited.

NURSES: *Pierre, Pierre!*

Pierre looks at the nurses. He looks at them for a long time. One nurse goes out of the room and says, 'Doctor, doctor, come quickly! Pierre is here again – his eyes are open!'
In the room, Pierre is lost. His eyes are open and they have many questions in them, but they are the eyes of a lost boy, a boy lost in time.
Questions start to come from his mouth – questions, questions, questions.

PIERRE: Is Olga OK?

DOCTOR: Who's Olga? Pierre, you are in hospital.

PIERRE: What did you say? Hospital? Am I ill? Where's my father?

DOCTOR: There's time for questions, Pierre, but not now. This is the beginning of your new life and it's your birthday today. Happy birthday!

PIERRE: Where's my father?

DOCTOR: I'm sorry, Pierre, but he's not here.

PIERRE: Where is he?

DOCTOR: He's … he was very ill … and he …

PIERRE: No, no, he's OK! Please say he's OK!

DOCTOR: I'm sorry, Pierre.

PIERRE: I'd like a drink.

The nurse gets a Coca-cola.

DOCTOR: First we've got some things to do.

PIERRE: What things?

NURSE: Questions, questions, Pierre, not so fast!

She gives Pierre a magazine.

NURSE: Look at this magazine. Find some presents – it's your birthday.

Pierre is on the computer page of the magazine.

PIERRE: How much is this?

NURSE: It's expensive, Pierre.

PIERRE: What is 'Internet'? Where's my mother? I'd like to see my mother.

NURSE: Your mother?

PIERRE: Yes, where is she? I'd like to see my mother now, please.

The doctor and nurses don't know about Pierre's mother. They look tired. Pierre's questions do not stop.

PIERRE: How old am I?

NURSE: You're fourteen.

PIERRE: Pardon? Fourteen? No, I'm nine! Where's my mother? I'd like to see my mother. Now! Now! Now!

10

CLOTHES FOR WORK AND PLAY

1 Weekend activities present simple; frequency adverbs

A Make questions about people and their weekend activities.

Example: *Pete/watch TV*   *Does Pete watch TV at the weekend?*

1. Chris/watch TV

.... ?

2. Steve and Maria/watch TV

.... ?

3. Steve/go out with friends

.... ?

4. Pete and Chris/go out with friends

.... ?

5. Dave/work at home

.... ?

6. Pete and Jo/work at home

.... ?

7. Jo/play sport

.... ?

8. Pete and Steve/play sport

.... ?

B Now answer these 8 questions with the information from the table on page 54.

Example: *Does Pete watch TV at the weekend?*
            Yes, he sometimes watches TV at the weekend.

1. ....

2. ....

3. ....

4. ....

5. ....

6. ....

7. ....

8. ....

Activities	Pete	Chris	Steve	Jo	Maria	Dave
watch TV	sometimes	never	usually	never	usually	sometimes
go out with friends	sometimes	sometimes	usually	always	always	always
work at home	never	always	sometimes	never	sometimes	usually
play sport	always football	never	always football	sometimes tennis	never	usually football

2 Whose is it?

whose; possessive *'s*

Damien

Debbie

Martina

1 tennis racket

2 hat

3 helmet

4 jacket

5 car

6 shoes

Look at the picture and then write questions and answers like this:

1. *Whose tennis racket is this? It's Martina's tennis racket.*
2. ....
3. ....
4. ....
5. ....
6. ....

A Put the answers to Jackie's questions in the right place in the conversation.

> It really suits you.
> No, they look lovely.
> I'm fine. Wow! They're great jeans.
> Yes, I really like them!

JACKIE: Hi! How are you?

JULIE: (1) *I'm fine. Wow! They're great jeans.*

JACKIE: Do you think so?

JULIE: (2) ....

JACKIE: What about the colour?

JULIE: (3) ....

JACKIE: Do you think they're too short?

JULIE: (4) ....

B Now make up a conversation like this between Matt and Tom. Tom has a new jacket. It's bright green.

TOM: Hi, Matt. How are you?

MATT: (1) ....

TOM: (2) ....

MATT: (3) ....

TOM: (4) ....

MATT: (5) ....

TOM: (6) ....

MATT: (7) ....

4 Words with two parts

Fill the gaps in these sentences with a two-part word.
Take a word from *A* and a word from *B*.

Example: *Paul works in a shop. He's a* ..*shop assistant*............................... .

1. Michael Schumacher is a famous German ....
2. A: Do you like my ....?

   B: Yes, I do. It's not too short.
3. I like water sports. I go to the .... every day.
4. A: I'm very cold.

   B: Wear your ....
5. I'm a short person. .... shoes suit me.

A

high-   mini-   racing   shop   sweat   swimming

B

assistant   driver   heeled   pool   shirt   skirt

5 Word groups

Put the words in the box into six groups.

baseball   boots   cap   doctor   finger   garden   hat   mouth
nurse   park   sandals   tennis

Group	Example	
1.	golf	*baseball* ....
2.	fire-fighter	....
3.	shoes	....
4.	helmet	....
5.	beach	....
6.	hand	....

6 Wordsearch

Find 10 clothes words. Words can go up (↑), down (↓),
forwards (→), backwards (←) or diagonally (↘).

T	H	A	T	T	D	B	T
T	R	Y	P	I	R	L	E
R	S	O	T	U	E	O	K
I	L	A	U	S	S	U	C
H	P	Y	N	S	S	S	A
S	A	E	T	D	E	E	J
T	C	E	I	T	A	R	O
W	F	R	T	T	K	L	S

A Read this short letter. How old are Susanna's friends?

> Dear Maria,
> Thank you for your letter this morning. What a great surprise!
>
> And thanks for the birthday present. It's very nice of you. It's a lovely T-shirt, the colour blue really suits me. Is it Mexican?
>
> I'm sorry you're not here. There's a big party at my house tonight with about a hundred and fifty people. I usually like birthdays, but this year I'm 25 — that's very old. My friends are all about 21 or 22.
>
> Can you come to stay here next year? I hope so. Have a good summer holiday with your friends in Mexico. Say hello to your parents. Thanks again for the lovely present.
>
> Love,
> Susanna

B Now answer some more questions.

1. Whose birthday is it?

....

2. Who is the letter to?

....

3. Where does she live?

....

4. What is the birthday present?

....

5. Where is the birthday party?

....

6. How many people are there at the party?

....

7. How old is Susanna?

....

📟 Listen to Maria and Susanna on the phone. It's different from the letter. Write five differences on the letter.

Write a letter to a friend. Thank him or her for a birthday present.
Fill in the spaces and finish the sentences.

Dear ....
Thank you for your letter ....
And thank for the .... present.
  It's very nice of you. It's a lovely
.... — the colour
.... really suits me . Is it
.... ?
  I'm sorry you are ....
There is a big party at ....
tonight with about .... people.
I usually like birthdays, but this year I'm
.... — that's very old.
My friends are all about ....
  Can you .... next year?
I hope so. Have a good holiday with
.... in ....
Say hello to .... Thanks again
for the ....
Love,

....

Do you hear *I'd like* or *I like*? Listen to the recording and tick one of the boxes.

	I'd like	*I like*
1.	☐	☐
2.	☐	☐
3.	☐	☐
4.	☐	☐
5.	☐	☐
6.	☐	☐

11 Visual dictionary

Complete the visual dictionary for Unit 10 on page 81.

Lost in time — EPISODE 10

'The jeans suit you, Pierre,' says the nurse.
The nurse looks at Pierre. He has some new clothes – some jeans, a T-shirt, and a baseball cap.
'I like jeans,' says Pierre, but I usually wear shorts. When is the plane?
'This afternoon,' says the nurse, 'don't worry.'

Pierre thinks of the plane to the Czech Republic and has a picture in his head of his mother at the airport in Prague. In this picture, his mother says: 'I love you, my wonderful son' and they are very happy. Pierre knows the picture is too good but he likes it very much.

At the airport Pierre is already tired. After so many years in bed in his personal, lost world, people are a problem, especially lots of people in loud places. One of the nurses is with Pierre.

A woman in a uniform speaks. 'Whose suitcase is this?'
'It's Pierre's,' says the nurse, 'and my suitcase is the blue one.'
The woman in uniform says, 'I like your teddy bear!'

Pierre has a little teddy bear for his mother. He still has the picture of his mother in his head.
'Open your eyes, Pierre,' says the nurse.

They start to get on the plane. Next to Pierre there is a young man in tennis shorts and a tennis shirt, and a woman in a mini-skirt. Pierre closes his eyes.

They are in the air. The nurse says to Pierre, 'Pierre, there is something I want to talk about. It's about your mother.'
'Yes?' says Pierre.
'We don't know where your mother is,' says the nurse. 'Perhaps she is not in Prague. Don't forget it's five years. We can go to the police and ask for help to find your mother. But don't forget, five years is a long time!'
'My father is dead. I know that now, but my mother is there. I know she is,' says Pierre.

He starts to get another picture in his head. A wonderful picture. His mother is there, she really is, not at the airport this time but in a big building – he knows the building. She is there in the building. But where is the building? He closes his eyes. Where is it?

11

ARE YOU THE RIGHT PERSON FOR YOUR JOB?

1 Job and business crossword

vocabulary

Across
2. An important person in a hospital
5. A learner in a university
6. A business
8. You read these in a newspaper,
   for jobs or accommodation

Down
1. A place for your money
3. A room inside a building for some workers
4. Money for work
7. A person with a top position

2 Answer for you

questions/short answers with *can*

Write answers to the questions for you with *Yes, I can* or *No, I can't.*

1. Can you write good letters? ....

2. Can you read English books? ....

3. Can you speak on the phone in English? ....

4. Can you fly a plane? ....

5. Can you eat spicy food? ....

6. Can you understand these questions? ....

3 Match A and B

questions and answers

Match the questions (*A*) with an appropriate answer (*B*).

A
1. Why do you like computers?
2. Why do you think your English course is interesting?
3. Why do you like your job?
4. Why are job interviews hard?

B
a. Because the teacher is good and the students are nice.
b. Because it's interesting and the people in my office are nice.
c. Because they keep a lot of information.
d. Because the people ask a lot of difficult questions.

A Look at adverts A and B quickly and answer questions 1–3.

1. What are the jobs in A and B?
2. In which countries are the jobs in A and B?
3. How many jobs are there in A and B? 2/4/5

A

C21 MANAGERS

Project Managers

Four key positions

Large international engineering company wants four special managers for its projects in Saudi Arabia.

Duties:
- manage one of four important projects in Saudi Arabia
- manage reporting systems
- manage about 50 project workers in each project

Skills/abilities:
- good management experience
- speak Arabic
- good with people from other countries
- good engineering qualifications
- computing skills

Salary: $80–90,000

Conditions: free accommodation
free air travel home 2 times a year
2-year contract

For more information, phone: 45838 2354.
Applications by 5 p.m., May 31st to:

Deborah White, CEO, Atlas Engineering
GPO Box 4162, New York, USA

B

Bookwise Booksellers

Bookshop Manager

Bookwise has got a key position in its new exciting bookshop and coffee shop in the centre of Toronto, Canada. This is an excellent opportunity for an experienced bookshop manager with good selling and people skills.

Please apply in writing to:
General Manager
Bookwise
GPO Box 1248
Toronto 112

B Answer these questions.

1. Which job has got free accommodation? Job ....
2. Does job B talk about salary? Yes/No
3. Is job A for a person with a second language? Yes/No
4. Do you think job A is for a very young engineer? Yes/No
5. Do you think job B is good for a friendly person? Yes/No

5 Interview questions

Here are some answers from an interview for job A. Write the questions.

Questions	Answers
1. *Do you speak Arabic?*	No, not Arabic, but I speak Spanish very well.
2.	Yes, I like Saudi Arabia very much – my brother lives there.
3.	Yes, salary is important, but an interesting job is important too.
4.	Yes, of course I do, everyone knows your company, because it's so big.
5.	No. July is not possible but I can start in September.

6 Why? Why not?

Listen to three conversations. People are talking about their jobs. In each conversation there is a *Why?* question and a *Why not?* question. Write the names of the jobs and complete the *because* answers under *Why?* and *Why not?*

Job	Why?	Why not?
1.	because it's	maybe because a lot of .... are ....
2.	because young people .... things all the time	because I ...., they're wonderful.
3.	because they go to	because some places are ....

Complete four excuses for the man and woman.

2 *We'd love to come but the* ....

3 *Sorry, Jean but we've got* ....

1 *I'm sorry, we can't , the car's at the garage* .

4 *I'm sorry, but we've got a* ....

▭ Listen to some answers.

8 Visual dictionary

Complete the visual dictionary for Unit 11 on page 82.

Lost in time – EPISODE 11 ▭

The nurse and Pierre go to the central police station in Prague. A policeman speaks some English.

NURSE: *Do you remember a letter from Ireland about a lost mother? We have got an appointment with your chief of police at 10 o'clock.*
POLICEMAN: *One moment, please.*

He walks to another room. A few minutes go by. Pierre is excited.

POLICEMAN: *Come this way, please.*

They go into a room. The chief of police is there. He is a big man but he looks kind. The first policeman stays to help with the English. They talk for a long time. The police are sorry, but it's difficult to find someone after so many years.
Pierre is lost in the picture in his head. He gets up and goes to the door.
'What's the matter?' asks the nurse.
'Nothing,' Pierre says, 'I want to go to the toilet.'
'It's outside, the second door,' says the policeman.
'Thanks,' says Pierre.

Outside the room he walks past the toilet and out into the street. He wants to find the place in the picture, the picture in his head.

'I can't speak Czech but I can walk', Pierre thinks. So he walks. He walks down old streets, past beer houses, churches, an old clock with tourists and cameras. He walks past a park. In his head the park makes a new picture, he hears his mother. She's in the park with the old man and the music, and the hot dogs. The building in the picture in his head is the hotel ... in the picture it's now very easy to see the hotel ... it's near the park, near here.

Pierre is excited. He walks quickly now for three or four minutes and then in a little street there it is – the hotel.

He goes into the hotel. It's different. The colours are now white and green, not white and brown. Pierre walks up to reception.

PIERRE:	*Do you speak English?*
RECEPTIONIST:	*A little, yes. Can I help you?*
PIERRE:	*I want my mother.*
RECEPTIONIST:	*Is she a visitor, I mean a guest here?*
PIERRE:	*No, no.*
RECEPTIONIST:	*Then why are you here?*
PIERRE:	*Because ... because I want my mother. We were here, my mother and I five years ago.*
RECEPTIONIST:	*Well, it's different here now, and not many guests stay for five years, you know.*
PIERRE:	*I know, I know. But in my picture ...*
RECEPTIONIST:	*Picture? Can I see it?*
PIERRE:	*Oh ... it doesn't matter.*

Then the young woman asks for his mother's name and looks up and down the list of guests at the hotel.

RECEPTIONIST:	*No, she's not here. I'm sorry. What about an advertisement in the paper? It's expensive, but perhaps your mother is in Prague somewhere.*
PIERRE:	*That's a good idea, thank you.*
RECEPTIONIST:	*It's OK, bye.*

Pierre is very sad. He walks past some people with suitcases, past the hotel lift and past a room with 'Private' on the door. Then he stops. He stops because he hears something ... but is it just something in his head?

Unit 11 ARE YOU THE RIGHT PERSON FOR YOUR JOB?

LET'S HAVE A PARTY

A Fill the gaps in the conversation with words and phrases from the box.

fantastic music	good idea	Let's go	See you later	too big
too early	too expensive	What about	What time	Where

RAYMUNDO: Are you busy tonight?

MARTA: No, I'm not.

RAYMUNDO: OK. (1) ....*Let's go*.............. for a meal.

MARTA: Great idea! (2) ....?

RAYMUNDO: The Metropolitan Hotel?

MARTA: No, it's (3) .... What about the new

               Japanese restaurant?

RAYMUNDO: No, Japanese food is (4) .... I haven't got much money.

MARTA: A fast food place, then?

RAYMUNDO: That's a (5) .... What about Express Pizza?

               The food is good, it isn't expensive and they play (6) ....

MARTA: That sounds great. (7) ....?

RAYMUNDO: Seven o'clock.

MARTA: That's (8) .... for me. Let's go at nine o'clock.

RAYMUNDO: No, that's too late. I usually eat before nine. (9) ....

               eight o'clock or half past eight?

MARTA: OK, let's say half past eight.

RAYMUNDO: OK. (10) ....

MARTA: Right. Bye, then.

💿 Listen to the recording and check your answers.

B  Listen again and answer these questions.

1. Where do they eat? (Tick ✓ the place.)
2. What's wrong with the other two places? (Write in the spaces.)

3. What time do they eat? (Tick ✓ the clock.)
4. What's wrong with the other times? (Write in the spaces.)

---

2 Join in the conversation

listening and speaking

A Listen to the recording. Reply to the suggestions. Reply with the ideas you hear.

B Listen again and write your answers here.

1. ....
2. ....
3. ....
4. ....

---

3 Where?

here or *there*

Fill the gaps in these sentences with *here* or *there*.

1. (On the telephone)

   A: Hello, this is Paula. Is Jessica ......*there*......, please?

   B: No, she isn't .... Sorry.

2. A: Can you come to my party?

   B: Where is it?

   A: It's .... at my house.

3. A: Welcome to London.

   B: I'm pleased to be ....

4. Is .... a theatre in your town?

5. A: .... are your keys.

   B: Thanks very much.

6. A: Do you know New York?

   B: No, I don't. Let's go ....

4 Wordsearch

Find the names of ten countries. Words can go up (↑),
down (↓), forwards (→), backwards (←) or diagonally (↗ ↘).

G	C	F	R	A	N	C	E	A
E	Y	H	X	S	T	Y	N	T
R	L	V	I	H	U	I	S	T
M	A	R	F	N	T	C	P	P
A	T	B	U	N	A	I	A	Y
N	I	G	E	W	A	C	I	G
Y	R	G	K	U	S	A	N	E
S	R	B	P	O	L	A	N	D
A	V	I	E	T	N	A	M	A

5 Words with two parts

Fill the gaps in these sentences with a two-part word. Take a word from *A* and a word from *B*.

A

birthday	business	conference	newspaper	shopping	university

B

journalist	list	meeting	party	room	student

1. A: Let's go to the supermarket and buy some food for the party.

   B: OK. Have you got the ..... *shopping list* ....?

2. Thanks for the invitation to your .... How old are you?

3. I'm a .... I write for the *New York Times*.

4. A: Are you a ....?

   B: Yes, I'm at Harvard. The teachers are good but it's hard work.

5. I'm sorry I can't come to your party. I've got a .... in
   our Paris office.

6. The meeting is in the large .... because a lot of people
   want to come.

6 Useful verbs

Fill the gaps in these sentences with the correct verb from the box.

go	have	make	see

1. I usually .... *go* .... shopping on Friday evening.

2. I always .... fun at parties.

3. Let's .... plans for our holiday.

4. A: .... a nice day.

   B: OK. .... you later.

5. A: Do you .... to work on Saturdays?

   B: No, I usually .... my friends.

6. What time do you .... breakfast?

7 Jumbled words

Read the clues and find the words.

Example: *Some people live here.* ___House___ (EHUSO)

1. A red or white drink .... (NEWI)
2. Mother and father .... (STRAPEN)
3. A is the beginning. Z is the .... (DEN)
4. Sons and daughters .... (NILCHERD)
5. In a short time .... (OSNO)

8 Spot the mistakes

There are ten mistakes in this reply to a party invitation. There are missing words and wrong words. Mark the mistakes.

> Dear Sylvie,
> Thanks you for the invitation your berthday party in Friday night.
> I want be their with you and our friends but I can come. I sorry but me mother is not very well.
> Have great time. See you next week.
> Love,
>
> Amanda

Now write the note again with no mistakes.

Dear Sylvie,

....

....

....

....

Love,

Amanda

9 Invitations

A Put the invitation words into the right place on the invitation.

231465	a bottle of something	At	At	birthday	friend	From	
my	On	Phone	To				

(1) .... *To* .... Jonathan

(2) .... Joe

It's (3) .... (4) .... party.

(5) .... Saturday 17 May

(6) 20.30

(7) .... The Beach Café

Bring a (8) .... and (9) ....

Can you come? (10) .... me. Tel.

(11) ....

B Now write an invitation to your birthday party.

....

....

It's .... party

....

....

....

Bring a .... and ....

Can you come? ....me. Tel. ....

10 Sounds

A Which sound is in these words – /s/ or /z/? Tick the boxes.

	/s/	/z/
1. busy	☐	☐
2. this	☐	☐
3. case	☐	☐
4. please	☐	☐
5. music	☐	☐
6. us	☐	☐
7. course	☐	☐
8. is	☐	☐

B ▭ Now listen to these words in sentences. Check your answers.

11 Visual dictionary

Complete the visual dictionary for Unit 12 on page 83.

Lost in time – EPISODE 12 ◑

Inside the room with 'Private' on the door, Pierre hears his name. The conversation is in Czech but he hears his name, 'Pierre'. A woman in a green and white hotel uniform comes out of the room. She has a drink and an ice cream on a tray. She is a room service waitress.

She walks past Pierre. He says one word: 'Mum?' She looks back at Pierre and drops the tray. Everyone stops and looks at the woman and the boy.

She speaks first in Czech. Pierre doesn't understand, but he looks at her eyes. They say everything. Then she speaks in English.

JANA: Pierre, no, no it can't be. Pierre?
PIERRE: Mum, you're here! The picture in my head is real … it's really you!

Mother and son are together and the lost love, the lost life of five years can start again. Pierre's mother is excited and asks question after question.

JANA: Where is your father?
PIERRE: He's not here. He's … dead.

Jana is white.

JANA: How?
PIERRE: I don't know really, a bad illness, I think. Why are you here after five years?
JANA: For years, the phone calls to and from Ireland, your father said, 'Don't come to Ireland; the police here want you'. I had no money, no friends. The job at the hotel is good because here I can remember our time in Prague and I've got some money. So I work and I wait, I work and I wait and every night in my little flat, I say: 'Pierre please come back to your mother'. Every night! Now today you are here! It's so wonderful. OK, so how about a drink and an ice cream?
PIERRE: Yeah, good idea!
JANA: We can sit over there.

They sit at a table; the ice cream arrives.

PIERRE: My first ice cream for five years!
JANA: Five years? But you love ice cream. My poor boy … your father was so …
PIERRE: No, no. It's not because of father. It's … it's a long story!
JANA: OK, tell me your story, because now we've got all the time in the world! We are not lost in time any more.

VISUAL DICTIONARY

LETTERS AND NUMBERS

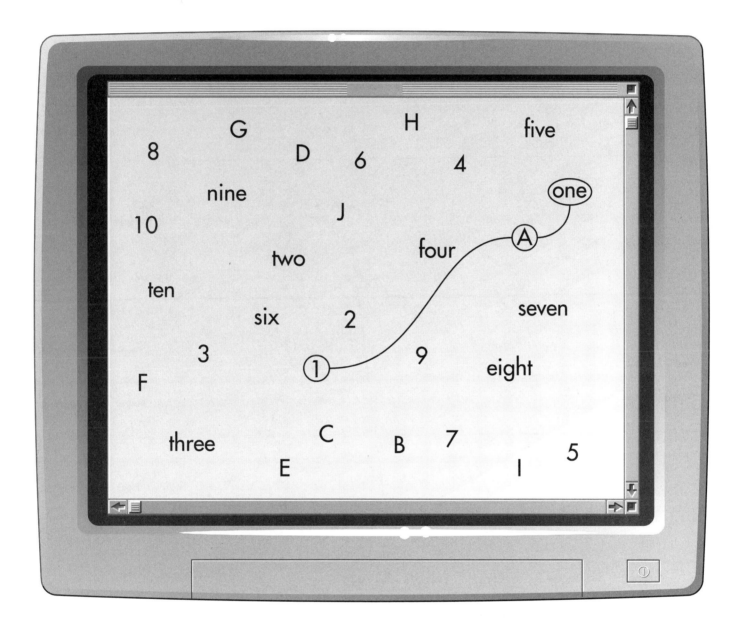

Join the numbers 1–10 with the correct word one–ten and with the letters A–J.

MORE NEW WORDS

....

....

....

....

....

COUNTRIES OF THE WORLD

Write the countries from the box on the map.

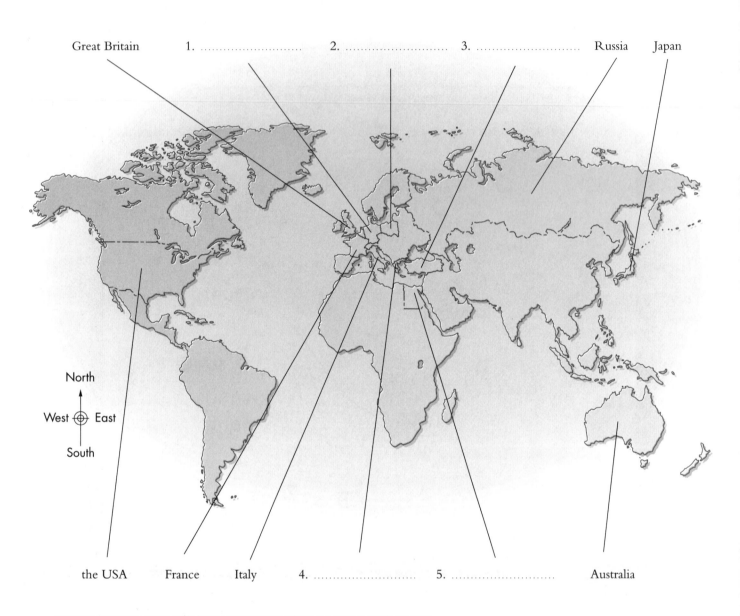

Great Britain   1. ....   2. ....   3. ....   Russia   Japan

North

West ⊕ East

South

the USA   France   Italy   4. ....   5. ....   Australia

| Egypt | Germany | Greece | Poland | Turkey |

Find *your* country. Write the name.

MORE COUNTRIES

Write the numbers on the map. Write the countries here.

....

....

....

....

....

POSSESSIONS

Write the words from the box under the pictures.

| a mobile phone | a cat | flowers | a letter |
| a magazine | a car | | |

a watch

1. ....

a ring

earrings

2. ....

3. ....

a book

A. JONES
BUILDER
14 YORK ST.
YOUR TOWN
ANY SHIRE
AN 1 02P   TEL/FAX
10134 6141

a business card

keys

4. ....

5. ....

6. ....

MORE NEW WORDS

....
....
....
....
....

IN THE CITY

Write the missing words.

1. ....

2. ....

castle   shops   station   cathedral

sports centre

3. ....

swimming pool   police station   hotel   4. ....

| bank | cinema | library | nightclub |

MORE NEW WORDS

....
....
....
....
....

AT HOME

Write the missing words.

bedroom

1. ....

bathroom

2. ....

picture

bookshelves

clock

living room

wife

son

5. ....

4. ....

wall

3. ....

| daughter | husband | kitchen | toilet | window |

MORE NEW WORDS

IN A HOTEL ROOM

Write the words for the things in the picture.

plane   1. ....   2. ....   3. ....   bed

4. ....   table   5. ....   passport   6. ....   7. ....

| bin | camera | lamp | safe | sunglasses | ticket | wardrobe |

MORE NEW WORDS

....

....

....

....

....

JOBS AND TIMES

Jobs

Write the missing words.

1. I'm a ....

2. I'm a ....

3. I'm a ....

4. I'm a ....

5. I'm a ....

6. I'm a ....

7. I'm a ....

8. I'm a ....

9. I'm an ....

10. I'm an ....

11. I'm a ....

| architect | doctor | engineer | journalist | lawyer | nurse |
| photographer | scientist | teacher | travel agent | waiter |

Times

1. He .... at ....
2. He .... at ....
3. He .... to work at ....
4. He .... work at ....
5. He .... home at ....

get	get up	go
have breakfast	start	

MORE NEW WORDS

....
....
....
....
....

FOOD

Write the names of the food with words from the box.

coffee 1. .... 2. .... 3. .... 4. .... 5. ....

6. .... 7. .... sandwich **8.** .... rice fish

| bananas | bread | cheese | chicken | oranges | salad | strawberries | wine |

MORE NEW WORDS

....

....

....

....

....

A STUDENT'S ROOM

Write the words.

2. ....   1. ....

4. ....   3. ....

5. ....

6. ....

7. ....

8. ....

9. ....

10. ....

11. ....

12. ....

13. ....

14. ....

15. ....   16. ....   17. ....   18. ....   19. ....

books	CDs	clock	credit card	desk	fridge	jeans	keys
lamp	magazine	necklace	painting	pen	personal stereo
postcard	shoes	telephone	umbrella	wallet

MORE NEW WORDS

....

....

....

....

....

CLOTHES

Write the words.

2. ....
1. ....
9. ....
10. ....
3. ....
4. ....
11. ....
5. ....
12. ....
6. ....
13. ....
14. ....
7. ....
8. ....
16. ....
15. ....

| blouse | cap | dress | flat shoes | hat | high-heeled shoes | pullover | shirt |
| shoes | shorts | skirt | suit | sweatshirt | T-shirt | tie | trousers |

17. ....

18. ....
19. ....

| boots | helmet | jacket |

MORE NEW WORDS

....
....
....
....
....

IN AN OFFICE

Write the missing words.

1. ....   notice board   2. ....   3. ....   4. ....

5. ....   application form   letter   office   business report   desk

| bin   chair   computer   interview   job advertisement |

MORE NEW WORDS

....

....

....

....

....

LET'S HAVE A PARTY

Write the words.

dance	drink	eat	sleep	talk

1. Some people ....

2. Some people ....

3. Some people ....

4. Some people ....

5. Some people ....

Party food

1. ....   2. ....   3. ....   4. ....   5. ....   6. ....

7. ....   8. ....   9. ....   10. ....   11. ....   12. ....   13. ....

beer	bread	cheese	chicken	cola	coffee	fruit	ham
rice	salad	sandwiches	water	wine			

MORE NEW WORDS

....

....

....

....

....

TAPESCRIPTS

1 HI AND BYE

2 I'm *fine*

1.
MAN: Morning.
WOMAN: Morning.

2.
MAN 1:   Hello. How are you?
MAN 2:   Fine. How are you?
MAN 1:   OK, thanks.

3.
WOMAN 1: Nice day.
WOMAN 2: Mm, beautiful.

4.
BOZENA: Hi, I'm Bozena. Are you Katerina?
KATERINA: Hi. Yes.

4 How are you?

1.
A: How are you?
B: Fine, thanks.

2.
A: Are you Juan?
B: No, I'm Jaime.

3.
A: I'm fine thanks. How are you?
B: I'm OK, thank you.

4.
A: What's your name?
B: Helena.
A: Am I late?
B: No, you're not.

8 Are you OK?

ELENA: Are you OK?
SANDOR: Yes, thanks.
ELENA: I'm Elena.
SANDOR: Pleased to meet you. I'm Sandor.
ELENA: Nice day.
SANDOR: Mm, and the coffee is good.
ELENA: Mm, it is.
SANDOR: It's a great coffee shop.
ELENA: Mm, it's nice.

2 WELCOME!

9 Join in the conversation

1. Hi, how are you?
2. I'm Jane. What's your name?
3. And what's your family name?
4. How do you spell that?
5. What's your address?

10 Sounds

1. Is that a hotel?
2. What's your address?
3. Welcome to New York.
4. Reception. Becky here.
5. Can I have a coffee, please?
   Yes, certainly.

11 Sounds tricky

1. It's the fourth floor not the fifth or the third.
2. It's the sixth station, not the second or the seventh.

3 PEOPLE AND THINGS IN MY LIFE

3 Yes, she is

1.
A: Is her husband OK?
B: Yes, he is, he's fine.

2.
A: Is her manager interesting?
B: Yes, she is, I think.

3.
A: Are her colleagues nice?
B: Yes, they are, very nice.

4.
A: Is this ring from Peru?
B: Yes, it is, from Lima.

5.
A: She's his wife?
B: Yes, she is. She's his second wife.

6 Thanks for the ...

1.
A: Hi.
B: Hi, thanks for the photograph.
A: You're welcome.

2.
A: Hello. How are you?
B: Fine. Oh, thank you for the letter.
A: You're welcome.

3.
A: Thanks very much for that ring, it's nice.
B: Don't mention it.

4.
A: Is that the phone book?
B: Yes, here you are.
A: Thanks very much.

4 ABOUT TOWN

9 Join in the conversation

What's your address?
Is your town in the south of the country?
Is it big?
Are there a lot of people?
Is it an old town?
Really, that's very interesting.

10 Sounds

A
1. age   thank   am   bad
2. two   you   do   house
3. are   bank   map   thanks
4. his   city   think like
5. sell   key   get   west

B
1. He's a famous man.
2. It's an old museum.
3. We're at a music festival.
4. That's a very modern cathedral.
5. She's a very important woman.

5 I'VE GOT ONE ON THE WALL

2 Clocks at home?

A: Have you got any clocks in your home?
B: No.
A: Really? We've got some.
B: Have you?
A: Mm. We've got a clock in the kitchen, one in the living room and one in the bathroom.
B: Any in the bedroom?
A: No, we haven't got any in our bedroom.
B: My sister's got some clocks in the toilet.
A: Where?

4 Mini conversations

1.
A: I'm tired.
B: Go to bed then.

2.
A: I've got a headache.
B: Have you? Take some tablets.

3.
A: Good night.
B: Good night. See you in the morning.

5 Two flats

Conversation 1, Flat 1
A: There's a flat in Mile End.
B: Oh, yes? How many bedrooms?
A: Two, and a new bathroom and kitchen.
B: Really? Sounds great.
A: It's £250 a week.
B: £250? We haven't got £250.
A: I know.

Conversation 2, Flat 2
A: Here's one ... Hendon.
B: That's OK.
A: Two bedrooms, new bathroom and TV.
B: Near the shops?
A: Yes, near the shops and train station.
B: Sounds fine.
A: Mm. £175 a week.
B: Really? That's not bad. Write down the phone number.
A: OK, got a pen?
B: Yeah, here you are.
A: Thanks.

6 DON'T FORGET YOUR SUNGLASSES

5 Where are my sunglasses?

WOMAN: Where are my sunglasses?
MAN: They're by the suitcase.
WOMAN: What about my camera?
MAN: It's in the suitcase.
WOMAN: Good. Is my passport there?
MAN: Yes, on the chair.
WOMAN: And my CDs?
MAN: They're under the chair.
WOMAN: OK. Thanks.

6 Days of the week

When are we going to the cinema?
When's the meeting?
And the visit to the library?
What day are we at the university?
And when's the disco?
When is dinner at the restaurant?
And the trip to the police station?
Oh, and that conference. What day is that?

7 TIME FOR WORK

9 Join in the conversation

Have you got the time, please?
Thanks very much. What's your job?
Oh, really? Where do you work?
Is it an interesting job?
And what time do you get up in the morning?

8 INTERNATIONAL FOOD

2 I like Indian food. Do you?

A: I like Indian food.
B: Do you?
A: Mm, it's great.

A: I don't like English food.
B: Don't you?
A: No, it's not very nice.

A: My mother likes Thai food.
B: Does she?
A: Yes, she eats it a lot.

A: They love sandwiches.
B: Do they?
A: Mm, very much.

A: My fish likes bread.
B: Does it?
A: Yes, it eats a lot of bread.

A: We don't like black coffee.
B: Don't you?
A: No, it's very strong.

A: My brother likes rice.
B: Does he?
A: Yes, he loves it.

6 Asking and answering

1. How are you?
2. What's your first name?
3. How long is your English course?
4. When is your birthday?
5. How many days are there in July?
6. Do you like Indian food?

7 I love fish

DANIELLA: Oh, hi, Paul.
PAUL: Hello, Daniella. Nice restaurant.
DANIELLA: Mm. Menu?
PAUL: Thanks.
DANIELLA: The fish is nice here.
PAUL: Is it? Mm ... I don't like fish.
DANIELLA: Really? I do. I love fish. What about curry then?

PAUL: OK ... Thai or Indian curry.
DANIELLA: I like Thai curry.
PAUL: Mm, so do I, and I like Indian curry.
DANIELLA: Do you? Mmm, I don't like Indian curry much, but I like Indian bread.
PAUL: Mm, me too, and rice.
DANIELLA: Oh yes, so do I.
WAITRESS: Ready to order?
PAUL: Yes.
DANIELLA: Yes, I think so.
PAUL: Erm, I'd like the Thai ...

9 MONEY! MONEY! MONEY!

8 Prices on the phone

A: Hello. Telephone sales. Can I help you?
B: Oh, yes, hello. I'd like some things from your catalogue, please.
A: What would you like?
B: I'd like a box of computer disks, please.
A: What's the catalogue number?
B: It's 170702.
A: 170702. That's £28.
B: Pardon?
A: £28.

B: Thank you. And I'd like a calculator.
A: One Casio calculator.
B: That's catalogue number 124302.
A: Thank you. That's £19.
B: Sorry, could you repeat that, please?
A: Yes, it's nineteen pounds.

B: And I'd like a chair, please.
A: A desk chair?
B: Yes, please.
A: What's the catalogue number?
B: It's 228789. I'd like a blue one, please.
A: OK, that's £74.
B: Pardon?
A: Seventy-four pounds.

A: Would you like anything else?
B: Yes, have you got a box of fifty black pens?
A: Yes, we have. That's catalogue number 130193.
B: 130193. How much is that?
A: Eight pounds.
B: Eighteen pounds?
A: No, eight pounds.
B: Thank you.

B: That's all, thanks.
A: Right. That's £129.
B: What did you say?
A: £129. How do you want to pay?
B: Credit card. Is that OK?
A: Fine. What's your card number ...

10 CLOTHES FOR WORK AND PLAY

8 On the phone

MARIA: Hi, Susanna?

SUSANNA: Yes, who's that?

MARIA: It's me, Maria.

SUSANNA: Where are you?

MARIA: I'm in Brazil.

SUSANNA: Oh, really. Listen, Maria, thanks for the red T-shirt. It's lovely.

MARIA: Oh, good. I'm glad you like it. When is your party?

SUSANNA: It's tonight.

MARIA: Where is it?

SUSANNA: It's at a restaurant in the town. There are 200 people.

MARIA: Great! How old are you this year?

SUSANNA: I'm twenty! That's terrible.

MARIA: Twenty isn't terrible. I'm twenty-five. That's terrible!

SUSANNA: Listen, Maria, can you come here next year?

MARIA: I think so.

SUSANNA: Great.

MARIA: OK. See you soon.

SUSANNA: Yes. Thank you for phoning and thanks for the present.

MARIA: OK. Bye.

SUSANNA: Bye.

10 *I'd like or I like?*

1. Wow! I like your hair!
2. I like red T-shirts.
3. Look. I'd like that black baseball cap.
4. These boots are really old. I'd like some new shoes for the summer.
5. That jacket really suits you. I like the colour.
6. I work very hard. I'd like a holiday.

11 ARE YOU THE RIGHT PERSON FOR YOUR JOB?

6 Why? Why not?

1.

A: What's your job?

B: I'm a nurse.

A: Do you like it?

B: Oh, yeah. It's a good job.

A: Why?

B: Because it's interesting. But a nurse's salary isn't very good.

A: Why not?

B: I don't know. Maybe because a lot of nurses are women.

2.

A: Teachers have got a difficult job.

B: Why do you say that?

A: Because young people like new things all the time.

B: Mmm. I don't think it's difficult.

A: Why not?

B: Because I like children, they're wonderful.

3.

A: Photographers have a great job.

B: Why?

A: Because they go to exciting places.

B: Mm. It's not always exciting.

A: Why not?

B: Well, because some places are dirty and people aren't always very friendly.

7 Sorry, the cat's ill

1.

JEAN: Hi.

MARIE AND GERARD: Hi, Jean.

JEAN: Can you come to dinner on Wednesday?

MARIE: Mm, I'm sorry we can't ... the car's in the garage.

JEAN: Oh, OK.

2.

JEAN: Hi.

MARIE AND GERARD: Hi, Jean.

JEAN: Can you come to dinner on Wednesday?

MARIE: We'd love to come but the cat's ill.

JEAN: Oh, OK.

3.

JEAN: Hi.

MARIE AND GERARD: Hi, Jean.

JEAN: Can you come to dinner on Wednesday?

GERARD: Sorry, Jean, but we've got our English class on Wednesday evening.

JEAN: Oh, OK.

4.

JEAN: Hi.

MARIE AND GERARD: Hi, Jean.

JEAN: Can you come to dinner on Wednesday?

GERARD: I'm sorry but we've got a meeting on Wednesday evening.

JEAN: Oh, OK.

12 LET'S HAVE A PARTY

1 Are you busy tonight?

RAYMUNDO: Are you busy tonight?

MARTA: No, I'm not.

RAYMUNDO: OK. Let's go for a meal.

MARTA: Great idea! Where?

RAYMUNDO: The Metropolitan Hotel?

MARTA: No, it's too big. What about the new Japanese restaurant?

RAYMUNDO: No, Japanese food is too expensive. I haven't got much money.

MARTA: A fast food place, then?

RAYMUNDO: That's a good idea. What about Express Pizza? The food is good, it isn't expensive and they play fantastic music.

MARTA: That sounds great. What time?

RAYMUNDO: Seven o'clock.

MARTA: That's too early for me. Let's go at nine o'clock.

RAYMUNDO: No, that's too late. I usually eat before nine. What about eight o'clock or half past eight?

MARTA: OK, let's say half past eight.

RAYMUNDO: OK. See you later.

MARTA: Right. Bye, then.

2 Join in the conversation

1. Let's go for a meal.
   YOU THINK THAT'S A GOOD IDEA. ASK WHERE.
2. What about the Burger Bar?
   SAY NO. YOU DON'T LIKE BURGERS.
3. Let's go to the Indian restaurant.
   SAY NO. YOU HAVEN'T GOT MUCH MONEY.
4. What about a Chinese meal, then?
   SAY YES. YOU LIKE CHINESE FOOD.

10 Sounds

1. Are you busy on Friday?
2. What's this?
3. Have you got a case?
4. Can I have a coffee, please?
5. Do you like music?
6. Tell us your address.
7. Of course I like swimming.
8. My T-shirt is blue.

ANSWER KEY

1 HI AND BYE

1 Hi

Possible answers

1. Hi!/Hello!   2. Fine, thanks.   3. Yes, very nice.   4. Hello, I'm ....., pleased to meet you.

2 I'm *fine*

1. morning
2. Hello   How are you?   fine   How are you?   OK, thanks.
3. nice day   Yes. Mm, it's a beautiful day
4. Hi, I'm Bozena, are you Katerina?   Hi. Yes

3 Correct the words

1. beautiful   2. eight   3. meeting   4. friend   5. teacher
6. letter

4 How are you?

1. How are you?   2. Are you   3. are you   4. What's your name? Am I

5 How about a coffee at ten?

Possible answer

Hi, Jean, I'm Tom. How are you?
It's a nice day. How about a coffee at ten?
My phone number is 0223 461250.
Bye
Tom Jones

6 It's a drink

Group word	Example
a drink	tea
a place	a park
a greeting	Hi.
a question	How are you?
a number	eight
a letter	K
a name	Laurence

7 26 letters in the alphabet

A a is letter number one (1)
J j is letter number ten (10)
C c is letter number three (3)
G g is letter number seven (7)
E e is letter number five (5)
I i is letter number nine (9)
D d is letter number four (4)

8 Are you OK?

1. thanks   2. meet   3. good   4. great   5. shop

9 Visual dictionary

1	one	A		6	six	f
2	two	B		7	seven	G
3	three	C		8	eight	H
4	four	D		9	nine	I
5	five	E		10	ten	j

2 WELCOME!

1 Matching

1. h   2. j   3. b   4. f   5. g (or a or i)   6. i   7. d   8. a (or c)
9. e   10. c

2 One, two, three

1. three men   2. six countries   3. two women   4. two buses
5. five floors   6. four people

3 Places

A

1. to   2. in   3. of   4. at (or in)   5. in   6. on

B

1. He's in London.
2. He's on the eighth floor.
3. He's in Australia.
4. He's at the Sheraton Hotel.

4 Correct the mistakes

1. Where's/Where **is** Bombay?
2. What's **that**?
3. France and Italy **are** in Europe.
4. My room is on the **sixth** floor.
5. Can **you** tell me your first name?
6. Can **I** help you?
7. Excuse **me**. Is this your key?
8. No, it **isn't**./**Yes**, it is.

5 Buildings, rooms and people

Buildings: bar   gym   hotel   restaurant   shop   station
Rooms: bar   gym   rest room   restaurant
People: friend   guide   student   teacher

6 Numbers and letters of the alphabet

A

NELSON MANDELA

B

1. 9, Heathfield Street, Liverpool, L6 3BJ
2. 00 33 3 22 25 68 63
3. RH1 6RF
4. kan3@dial.pipex.com
5. Schumacher

7 Countries, cities and towns

Countries:	Cities and towns:
Spain	Barcelona
Portugal	Lisbon
Israel	Tel Aviv
Greece	Athens
Turkey	Istanbul
USA	Denver
South Africa	Cape Town
Canada	Montreal
India	Calcutta
France	Paris
Australia	Melbourne
Germany	Berlin

9 Join in the conversation

1. (I'm) fine, thanks.
2. My name's ...
3. My family name's ...
4. ...
5. My address is ...

10 Sounds

1. ho**tel**
2. add**ress**
3. **wel**come
4. re**cep**tion
5. **cer**tainly

12 Visual dictionary

1. Germany   2. Poland   3. Turkey   4. Greece   5. Egypt

3 PEOPLE AND THINGS IN MY LIFE

1 They're about 3

1. He's about 20.   2. She's about 40.   3. We're 60.
4. They're about 3.   5. I'm ....   6. It's very old.

2 That's my business card

1. That's our little girl.   2. That's her letter.   3. That's their address book.   4. That's my business card.   5. That's his credit card.

3 Yes, she is

A
1. Yes, he is   2. Yes, she is   3. Yes, they are   4. Yes, it is
5. Yes, she is

B
Questions and answers with *is/are*
For questions with *Is he ...?* you answer *Yes/Yes, he is* or *No/No, he isn't.*
For questions with *Is she ...?* you answer *Yes/Yes, she is* or *No/No, she isn't.*
For questions with *Are you ...?* you answer *Yes/Yes, I am* or *No/No, I'm not.*
For questions with *Are they ...?* you answer *Yes/Yes, they are* or *No/No, they aren't.*

4 Is that his wife?

She's his **wife**?

6 Thanks for the ...

1. Photograph: thanks   2. Letter: thank you   3. Ring: thanks very much   4. Phone book: thanks very much

7 My friend

Possible answer
Helga is my friend. She's from Germany. She's nice.

8 Number crossword

Across: 2. hundred   4. eighty   6. sixty   8. seventy
Down: 1. thirty   3. ninety   5. thirteen   7. six

9 Visual dictionary

1. a mobile phone   2. flowers   3. a letter   4. a car   5. a cat
6. a magazine

4 ABOUT TOWN

1 Matching

1. Is; is
2. Are; aren't
3. any; are
4. a; isn't
5. Is; an; is
6. Are; any; aren't

2 In town

A *Possible answers*
Are there any shops in the town?
Is there a cinema in the town?
Are there any people in the town?
Are there ant telephones in the town?
Is there a café in the town?
Is there a theatre in the town?

3 How old are they?

Possible answers
1. The Pompidou Centre in Paris is over 20 years old.
2. The Empire State Building in New York is over 60 years old.
3. The New Shakespeare's Globe Theatre in London is two or three years old.
4. The Templo Sagrada Familia in Barcelona is around 115 years old.
5. The Catholic Cathedral in Liverpool is over 30 years old.
6. The Tokyo City Hall is around 10 years old.

4 Conversation

1. Where's this?
2. Is it a big city?
3. Really? That's very big.
4. How old is it?
5. Really? That's very old.

5 North, south, east, west

A
1. Melbourne is in the south of the country/Australia.
2. Perth is in the west of the country/Australia.
3. Darwin is in the north of the country/Australia.
4. Brisbane is in the east of the country/Australia.

6 Puzzles

A
1. university   2. sports centre   3. modern   4. station
5. million   6. library   7. hundred   8. thousand
The country is Scotland.

B
1. sixteen × seventeen = two hundred and seventy-two
2. twenty-one × fourteen = two hundred and ninety-four
3. eighty-nine × nineteen = one thousand six hundred and ninety-one
4. fifty-five × sixty-six = three thousand six hundred and thirty
5. two thousand × eleven = twenty-two thousand

7 Washington

1. capital   2. east   3. country   4. city   5. people   6. famous
7. parks

10 Sounds

A

1. age   2. house   3. are   4. like   5. key

B

1. famous   2. museum   3. festival   4. cathedral   5. important

11 Visual dictionary

1. cinema   2. nightclub   3. library   4. bank

5 I'VE GOT ONE ON THE WALL

1 He's got a sister

1. He's got a sister.
2. He's got a father and a mother. / He's got a wife and a son.
3. She's got a husband.
4. They've got a big family.

2 Clocks at home?

1. any   2. some   3. Any   4. any   5. some

3 A red letter day

1. green   2. white   3. blue   4. red   5. yellow

4 Mini conversations

1. A: I'm tired.   B: Go to bed then.
2. A: I've got a headache.   B: Have you? Take some tablets.
3. A: Good night.   B: Good night. See you in the morning.

5 Two flats

Flat 1: two bedrooms (not three); £250 a week (not £215)
Flat 2: new bathroom (not new kitchen); TV (not No TV)

6 Accommodation

A

Place	Accommodation	Price
West Lakes	Flat	$230
Kensington Gardens	House	$60
Enfield	Room	$50

B

1. No   2. Yes   3. Yes   4. No

8 Ask the person on the plane

Possible answers

1. Have you got any children?
2. Have you got a pen, please?
3. Have you got a magazine?
4. Has your company got an office in Paris?
5. Has your sister got a friend in Berlin?
6. Has your husband got a company in London?

9 Visual dictionary

1. toilet   2. window   3. kitchen   4. husband   5. daughter

6 DON'T FORGET YOUR SUNGLASSES

2 Go? Don't go?

1. Yes, go to Hungary this November.
2. No, don't take your camera on the tour.
3. Yes, stay at the Premier Hotel.

4. No, don't tell the travel agent about the hotel bedroom.
5. No, don't phone the tourist information office.

3 Travelling in London

1. Travel times.   2. 20 hours   3. No   4. No   5. No   6. Yes

5 Where are my sunglasses?

1. They're by the suitcase.
2. It's in the suitcase.
3. Yes, on the chair.
4. They're under the chair.

7 Visual dictionary

1. wardrobe   2. safe   3. bin   4. lamp   5. camera   6. ticket
7. sunglasses

7 TIME FOR WORK

1 Differences

1. My sister doesn't work in an office. She works in a shop.
2. I don't get up very early. I get up very late.
3. My brother doesn't have breakfast at 6 o'clock. He has breakfast at 7 o'clock.
4. I don't finish work at 11 o'clock at night. I finish work at 6 o'clock in the evening.
5. My sister doesn't watch television every evening. She watches television at the weekend.

2 People and their work

B

1. What's your name?
2. What's your job? or What do you do?
3. Where do you work?
4. When do you start work?
5. What time do you finish work?
6. What do you do in your shop / in your office / in your school?

C

1. My name's John.	My name's Mandi.
2. I'm a travel agent.	I'm a journalist.
3. I work in a shop in London.	I work in an office and at/in sports centres in Dublin.
4. I start work at nine o'clock in the morning.	I start work at one o'clock in the afternoon.
5. I finish work at six o'clock in the evening.	I finish work at eleven o'clock at night.
6. I serve customers.	I watch sports, interview people and write about sport.

D

Her name is Elaine. She is a teacher and she works in an English school in Egypt. She starts work at half past eight in the morning and (she) finishes (work) at a quarter past four in the afternoon. She teaches children between four and five years old /four–five years old.

3 Questions to answers

1. Where does he work?
2. What does she do?/What's her job?
3. What time/When do you get up (in the morning)?
4. Does she work in Washington?
5. Where do they live?
6. What time/When does he finish work?

4 What's the time?

A

1. 14.10
2. 02.30
3. 11.25
4. 13.45
5. 09.15
6. 23.55
7. 20.20
8. 19.05
9. 16.40
10. 07.35

B

5 Who does what where?

A

1. teacher	teach	school or university
2. doctor	help	people in hospital
3. waiter	serve	customers in a café
4. scientist	work	in a laboratory
5. businessperson	have	meetings in an office
6. journalist	write	in a newspaper

B

2. A doctor helps people in hospital.
3. A waiter serves customers in a café.
4. A scientist works in a laboratory.
5. A businessperson has meetings in an office.
6. A journalist writes in a newspaper.

6 Missing words

1. of   2. in   3. at   4. at   5. to   6. with   7. to   8. to
9. from   10. for

7 Puzzles

A

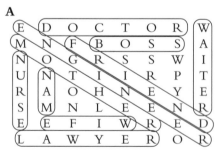

B

1. shop assistant   2. travel agent   3. university student
4. department store   5. living room   6. football stadium

8 Journeys

A

1. The travel agent is New Intertravel Ltd.
2. The customer is Mr P Jarvis.

B

2. My flight goes from Heathrow at five to four in the afternoon.
3. I get to Istanbul at a quarter to ten at night/in the evening.
4. I come back from Turkey on Saturday.

5. I check in at a quarter to eight in the morning.
6. I get back to London at eleven o'clock in the morning.

10 Visual dictionary

Jobs: 1. teacher   2. lawyer   3. scientist   4. nurse
5. photographer   6. waiter   7. travel agent   8. doctor
9. architect   10. engineer   11. journalist

Times: 1. He gets up at 6.30.   2. He has breakfast at 7.00.
3. He goes to work at 7.30.   4. He starts work at 8.15.
5. He gets home at 5.45.

8 INTERNATIONAL FOOD

2 I like Indian food. Do you?

See the tapescript on page 86.

3 Airline menu

1. True   2. False   3. True   4. False   5. False

4 Letter from a student in another country

1. and   2. but   3. but   4. and   5. but   6. and   7. and
8. and

5 Where's my new bag?

1. b   2. c   3. d   4. a   5. f   6. e

7 I love fish

Paul doesn't like fish. He likes Thai curry, Indian curry, Indian bread and rice.
Daniella doesn't like Indian curry. She likes fish, Thai curry, Indian bread and rice.

8 Visual dictionary

1. chicken   2. wine   3. bananas   4. oranges   5. cheese
6. bread   7. salad   8. strawberries

9 MONEY! MONEY! MONEY!

1 Going cheap

A

a. magazines   b. painting   c. camera   d. books   e. radio
f. bed   g. lamp   h. CDs   i. umbrella   j. suitcase   k. clock
l. fridge

B/C

1. How much does the bed cost?
   It costs thirty dollars.
2. How much are the books?
   They're one dollar each or five dollars for ten.
3. How much do the CDs cost?
   They cost two dollars each or ten dollars for six.
4. How much does the fridge cost?
   It costs twenty-five dollars.
5. How much is the lamp?
   It's twelve dollars.
6. How much are the magazines?
   They're two dollars for five.
7. How much does the painting cost?
   It costs two thousand dollars.
8. How much is the radio?
   It's twenty dollars.

9. How much is the suitcase?
   It's five dollars.
10. How much does the umbrella cost?
    It costs four dollars.

2 Shopping

Conversation 1
1. I'd like a T-shirt, please.
2. Have you got a green T-shirt / a green one?
3. Large, please./A large one, please.
4. How much is it?/How much does it cost?

Conversation 2
1. I'd like some shoes, please.
2. Thirty-eight/Forty-four.
3. Have you got brown (ones)?
4. Blue, please./The blue ones, please./I'd like (the) blue ones, please.
5. How much are they?/How much do they cost?
6. That's (very) cheap.

Conversation 3
1. I'd like an umbrella, please.
2. Have you got a black one?
3. Small, please./A small one, please.
4. How much are they?/How much do they cost?
5. That's very expensive. Can I have the small one/umbrella, please?

3 Questions and answers

A
1. What 2. How 3. What 4. Where 5. Who 6. How

B
1. f 2. d 3. c 4. e 5. a 6. b

4 Word lists

Money	Food	People
credit card	eat	actress
dollar	freezer	assistant
pay	fridge	boyfriend
price	lunch	children
wallet	snack	grandson

5 Word puzzle

1. cheap 2. peseta 3. wallet 4. snack 5. silver 6. toys
7. fridge 8. pounds 9. jewellery 10. catalogue

6 Choose some shoes

B
1. a. Yes b. Yes c. No d. Yes e. Yes f. No
2. a. £59.99 b. £49.99 c. £59.99 d. £49.99 e. £39.99

8 Prices on the phone

A/B

	Price	Catalogue number
1. Computer disks	£28	170702
2. Casio calculator	£19	124302
3. Desk chair	£74	228789
4. Box of black pens (50)	£8	130193
Total	£129	

9 Visual dictionary

1. painting 2. lamp 3. postcard 4. books 5. clock
6. CDs 7. magazine 8. credit card 9. wallet 10. necklace
11. telephone 12. desk 13. jeans 14. shoes 15. keys
16. personal stereo 17. fridge 18. umbrella 19. pen

10 CLOTHES FOR WORK AND PLAY

1 Weekend activities

A
1. Does Chris watch TV at the weekend?
2. Do Steve and Maria watch TV at the weekend?
3. Does Steve go out with (his) friends at the weekend?
4. Do Pete and Chris go out with (their) friends at the weekend?
5. Does Dave work at home at the weekend?
6. Do Pete and Jo work at home at the weekend?
7. Does Jo play sport at the weekend?
8. Do Pete and Steve play sport at the weekend?

B
1. No, he never watches TV at the weekend.
2. Yes, they usually watch TV at the weekend.
3. Yes, he usually goes out with (his) friends at the weekend.
4. Yes, they sometimes go out with (their) friends at the weekend.
5. Yes, he usually works at home at the weekend.
6. No, they never work at home at the weekend.
7. Yes, she sometimes plays tennis at the weekend.
8. Yes, they always play football at the weekend.

2 Whose is it?

Question	Answer
2. Whose hat is this?	It's Debbie's hat.
3. Whose helmet is this?	It's Damien's helmet.
4. Whose jacket is this?	It's Debbie's jacket.
5. Whose car is this?	It's Damien's car.
6. Whose shoes are these?	They're Martina's shoes.

3 Wow!

A
1. Fine. Wow! They're great jeans.
2. Yes, I really like them!
3. It really suits you.
4. No, they look lovely.

B
Possible answers
1. I'm fine. Wow! That's a great jacket.
2. Do you think so?
3. Yes, I really like it.
4. What about the colour?
5. It really suits you.
6. Do you think it's too big?
7. No, it looks great.

4 Words with two parts

1. racing driver
2. mini-skirt
3. swimming pool
4. sweatshirt
5. high-heeled

5 Word groups

1. golf   baseball   tennis
2. fire-fighter   doctor   nurse
3. shoes   boots   sandals
4. helmet   cap   hat
5. beach   garden   park
6. hand   finger   mouth

6 Wordsearch

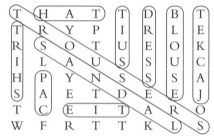

7 Thank you letter

A

Susanna's friends are 21 or 22.

B

1. It's Susanna's birthday.
2. It is to Maria (from Susanna).
3. She lives in Mexico.
4. It's a blue T-shirt.
5. The party is at Susanna's house.
6. There are about 150 people at the party.
7. Susanna is 25.

8 On the phone

Letter	Phone call
Maria is in Mexico.	Maria is in Brazil.
The T-shirt is blue.	The T-shirt is red.
The party is at Susanna's house.	The party is at a restaurant.
There are 150 people at the party.	There are 200 people at the party.
Susanna is 25.	Susanna is 20.

10 *I'd like or I like?*

	I'd like	*I like*
1.		✓
2.		✓
3.	✓	
4.	✓	
5.		✓
6.	✓	

11 Visual dictionary

1. shirt   2. tie   3. hat   4. pullover   5. suit   6. shorts
7. trousers   8. shoes   9. cap   10. blouse   11. dress
12. T-shirt   13. sweatshirt   14. flat shoes   15. high-heeled
shoes   16. skirt   17. helmet   18. jacket   19. boots

11 ARE YOU THE RIGHT PERSON FOR YOUR JOB?

1 Job and business crossword

Across: 2. doctor   5. student   6. company   8. adverts
Down: 1. bank   3. office   4. salary   7. manager

3 Match A and B

1. c   2. a   3. b   4. d

4 The job for you?

A

1. Project manager and Bookshop manager
2. Saudi Arabia and Canada
3. 5. Advert A has 4; Advert B has 1.

B

1. Job A
2. No
3. Yes
4. probably No
5. Yes

5 Interview questions

Possible questions

1. Do you speak Arabic?   2. Do you like Saudi Arabia?
3. Is (a good) salary important to you?   4. Do you know
(much about) our company?   5. Can you start in July?

6 Why? Why not?

1. Nurse	because it's interesting	maybe because a lot of nurses are women
2. Teacher	because young people like new things all the time	because I like children, they're wonderful
3. Photographer	because they go to exciting places	because some places are dirty and people aren't always very friendly

8 Visual dictionary

1. job advertisement   2. chair   3. bin   4. interview   5. computer

12 LET'S HAVE A PARTY

1 Are you busy tonight?

A

1. Let's go   2. Where?   3. too big   4. too expensive 5. good idea   6. fantastic music   7. What time   8. too early 9. What about   10. See you later

B

1. Express Pizza
2. The Metropolitan Hotel is too big. The Japanese restaurant is too expensive.
3. Half past eight.
4. Seven o'clock is too early. Nine o'clock is too late.

2 Join in the conversation

Possible answers

1. Great idea!/Good idea!/That's a great/good idea! Where?
2. No, I don't like burgers.
3. No, Indian food is too expensive (for me). I haven't got much money.
4. OK./Good idea. I like Chinese food.

3 Where?

1. there; here   2. here   3. here   4. there   5. Here   6. there

ACKNOWLEDGEMENTS

Authors' acknowledgements
We would like to thank the other series authors Ruth Gairns, Stuart Redman and Joanne Collie for their professionalism and continuing support as the *True to Life* series grows. Special thanks to Joanne Collie for her valuable feedback on early drafts of this material.

At Cambridge University Press our special thanks go to our commissioning editor, Kate Boyce, who has been a patient, courteous, and constant professional guide throughout the writing, feedback, revision and production process. To our editor, Helena Gomm, we are grateful for her tireless excellence in ensuring economy, consistency and accuracy. We are grateful also to Frances Amrani for editing the Teacher's Book, to Martin Williamson of Prolingua Productions and the staff at Studio AVP for producing the recordings, and to the design team, Samantha Dumiak and Gecko Limited.

Stephen Slater is grateful to his family for their patience and to the family dog for her unconditional enthusiasm for life, which has transferred valuable, positive energy to him when he really needed it.

The authors and publishers would like to thank the following individuals and institutions for their help in testing the material and for the invaluable feedback which they provided:
Laura Renart, T. S. Eliot Institute, Buenos Aires, Argentina; Pat MacRitchie, Hawthorn English Language Centre, Victoria, Australia; Judy D'All, Centre d'Anglais d'Angers, Angers, France; Don Ward, Centre d'Étude des Langues, Évry Cedex, France; Miriam Zeh-Glöckler, Sprachwerkstatt Glöckler, Leipzig, Germany; Kerry Flanagan, Regent Italia, Milan, Italy; Suzanne Wragge, Buckingham School, Rome, Italy; Michelle Hug, Rothrist, Switzerland; Canan O'Flynn, Bilgi University, Istanbul, Turkey.

The authors and publishers are grateful to the following illustrators and photographic sources:
Illustrators: David Axtell: pp. 6, 17, 19, 28; Phil Burrows: p. 9; Lee Ebrell: pp. 5, 10, 66; Martin Fish: p. 55; Steve Lach: pp. 4 *t*, 8, 15, 26, 30, 73 – 83; Mark McLaughlin: pp. 4 *b*, 25, 26, 32, 42, 62, 63, 65; Tracy Rich: pp. 46, 54; Jamie Sneddon: pp. 4, 6, 10, 15, 16, 17, 21, 25, 30, 31, 33, 37, 44, 54, 71, 72; John Storey: pp. 7, 13, 14, 18, 23, 24, 29, 33, 34, 40, 45, 51, 59, 64, 70.
Photographic sources: p. 15 *br* L.D. Gordon/Image Bank; p. 15 *bl* David Kampfner/Life File; p. 15 *tr*, *cl*, *tl*, 25, 35, 49, 54 *t*, David Simson; p. 20 *tl* Chris Parker/Axiom; p. 20 *tc* Alberto Arzoz/Axiom; p. 20 *tr* Darley/Edifice; p. 20 *bl* Steve J. Benbow/Axiom; p. 20 *bc* A.F. Kersting; p. 20 *br* Jim Holmes/Axiom; p. 27 Lewis/Edifice; p. 31 Jeremy Hoare/Life File; p. 54 *bl*, *br* Tony Henshaw/Action Plus; p. 54 *bc* Nigel French/Collections.

The authors and publishers are also grateful to the London Transport Museum for permission to reproduce material in 'Travelling in London' on page 31.

t = top, *b* = bottom, *c* = centre, *l* = left, *r* = right

Design and production by Gecko Ltd, Bicester, Oxon.
Picture research by Callie Kendall.
Sound recordings by Martin Williamson, Prolingua Productions, at Studio AVP, London.

4 Wordsearch

```
G  C  F  R  A  N  C  E  A
E  Y  H  X  S  T  Y  N  T
R  L  V  I  H  U  I  S  T
M  A  R  F  N  T  C  P  P
A  T  B  U  N  A  I  A  Y
N  I  G  E  W  A  C  I  G
Y  R  G  K  U  S  A  N  E
S  R  B  P  O  L  A  N  D
A  V  I  E  T  N  A  M  A
```

5 Words with two parts

1. shopping list
2. birthday party
3. newspaper journalist
4. university student
5. business meeting
6. conference room

6 Useful verbs

1. go   2. have   3. make   4. Have; See   5. go; see
6. have

7 Jumbled words

1. wine   2. parents   3. end   4. children   5. soon

8 Spot the mistakes

Dear Sylvie,

Thank you for the invitation **to** your **birth**day party **on** Friday
night. I want **to** be **there** with you and our friends but I **can't**
come. **I'm** sorry but **my** mother is not very well.
Have **a** great time. See you next week.
Love,
Amanda

9 Invitations

A
1. To   2. From   3. my   4. birthday   5. On   6. At   7. At
8. friend   9. a bottle of something   10. Phone   11. 231465

10 Sounds

	/s/	/z/
1. busy		✓
2. this	✓	
3. case	✓	
4. please		✓
5. music		✓
6. us	✓	
7. course	✓	
8. is		✓

11 Visual dictionary

1. drink   2. dance   3. eat   4. talk   5. sleep

Party food: 1. coffee   2. beer   3. bread   4. water   5. Coca-
Cola   6. wine   7. chicken   8. salad   9. cheese   10. fruit
11. sandwiches   12. rice   13. ham